Why
Johnny
Can't
Brand

24

Why Johnny Can't Brand

*Rediscovering
the Lost Art of
the Big Idea*

BILL SCHLEY

AND

CARL NICHOLS, JR.

Portfolio

For Len and Harriet, Carl Sr. and Joan,
to whom we owe everything

PORTFOLIO

Published by the Penguin Group

Penguin Group (USA) Inc., 375 Hudson Street, New York, New York 10014, U.S.A. • Penguin Group (Canada), 90 Eglinton Avenue East, Suite 700, Toronto, Ontario, Canada M4P 2Y3 (a division of Pearson Penguin Canada Inc.) • Penguin Books Ltd, 80 Strand, London WC2R 0RL, England • Penguin Ireland, 25 St. Stephen's Green, Dublin 2, Ireland (a division of Penguin Books Ltd) • Penguin Books Australia Ltd, 250 Camberwell Road, Camberwell, Victoria 3124, Australia (a division of Pearson Australia Group Pty Ltd) • Penguin Books India Pvt Ltd, 11 Community Centre, Panchsheel Park, New Delhi - 110 017, India • Penguin Group (NZ), Cnr Airborne and Rosedale Roads, Albany, Auckland 1310, New Zealand (a division of Pearson New Zealand Ltd) • Penguin Books (South Africa) (Pty) Ltd, 24 Sturdee Avenue, Rosebank, Johannesburg 2196, South Africa

Penguin Books Ltd, Registered Offices: 80 Strand, London WC2R 0RL, England

First published in 2005 by Portfolio, a member of Penguin Group (USA) Inc.

10 9 8 7 6 5 4 3 2 1

PUBLISHER'S NOTE

This publication is designed to provide accurate and authoritative information in regard to the subject matter covered. It is sold with the understanding that the publisher is not engaged in rendering legal, accounting or other professional services. If you require legal advice or other expert assistance, you should seek the services of a competent professional.

LIBRARY OF CONGRESS CATALOGING IN PUBLICATION DATA

Schley, Bill.
    Why Johnny can't brand : rediscovering the lost art of the big idea / Bill Schley and Carl Nichols, Jr.
        p. cm.
    Includes index.
    ISBN 1-59184-112-7
    1. Brand name products. 2. Brand name products—Marketing. 3. Brand name products—Management.
    I. Nichols, Carl, Jr. II. title.

    HD69.B7S3417 2005
    658.8'27—dc22   2005047664

Printed in the United States of America • Designed by Susan Hood

CONTENTS

Contents

Contents

Contents

INTRODUCTION
"HOUSTON (AND NEW YORK, CHICAGO, BOSTON) . . . WE HAVE A PROBLEM"

Most companies speak in generalities that "roll off the human understanding like water off a duck's back." But give me one Dominant Selling Idea—and that brand will pierce the fog like a headlight on a train.

Guru Mahatma Mahareshi "Mahesh" Goldberg

Some statistics you can't believe until you see them for yourself. For example, nobody in Manhattan, where everybody's thin, really believes that almost 60 percent of the population of America—winner of two world wars, sole superpower, and home of the brave—is now, officially, obese. But they do after they spend a day at Six Flags.

So when we tell CEOs and senior executives that there's a similar epidemic in American branding that's so acute, seven out of ten companies are going to market in the most cluttered conditions in history with formless positioning and flabby claims devoid of any differentiating punch; that record billions of dollars each year are being thrown out the window like confetti because of it; and that dominant brand identity for good companies has become American industry's #1 most valuable wasted asset, they don't always accept it.

Then we tell the following story. It illustrates the basic marketing problem so many good companies still haven't solved.

The Day Marketing Jumped the Guard Rail

A few short years ago, at the end of the millennium, there was a business phenomenon called the Dot-Com Disaster, a time when grown-ups gave billions to twenty-three-year-olds to start Internet companies without any visible demand or customers. If you were investing back then, you probably have no recollection of it now, something that's normal after a really bad accident. This era had a carry-over effect on the world of marketing. It reached a peak on January 30, 2000, a historic day. As it unfolded for all to see like a pile-up on a California freeway, it was miraculous. By God there it was, the grand finale—the end of business sanity as we know it—the *ads for Super Bowl XXXIV on TV.* By the second half, it was clear that if the state of American branding didn't improve soon, someone ought to write a book. We gave it a multiyear grace period.

It didn't.

For those of you this past year who saw the flatulent Budweiser Clydesdale lift his tail, ignite a gaseous emission and blast the makeup off the blonde's face—and wondered how that triggered a thirst for Bud—or who asked the question after seeing $75 million worth of advertising, "I know the Duck quacks but *what does the company do?*"—the classic examples from that historic Super Bowl are as illustrative today as they were then . . .

Singing Chimps and Rioting Brides

On that January day, you could watch as company after company gleefully wasted $4.2 million per minute of their shareholder's money and opportunity under the tutelage of the world's most respectable advertising agencies. Entertainment-wise it was an A+. We saw the famous sock puppet sing "If You Leave Me Now" by Chicago, mourning the fact that his master walked to the pet store instead of using the Web to order his Kibble. We saw cowboys herding cats on the open range for twenty-seven seconds while cowpoke after cowpoke tried to top the same cat-herding joke; until finally, in the last three seconds, the announcer revealed it was a commercial for EDS, who should now earn our business in integrated computing. Another appeal for our wallet share showed a dozen brides in white gowns start a fistfight at the stationery store because someone picked the same invitation. Best of all, we saw a dancing chimpanzee in an E*Trade T-shirt next to a couple of sad-sack investors who actually said, "Well, we just wasted our two million dollars. Now what?" Must have cast the client in that one.

In every ad, the average time for DOM (delivery of mirth) was twenty-five seconds. Average time of sales message: five seconds. Name on screen: two. Needless to say, viewers were highly amused, but almost no one could match an ad to a product. And no one cared. So much for 250 million bucks. So much for marketing execs making 500,000 dollars a year who are supposed to know better. The epidemic of sense-defying "branding," building for years, reached a crescendo that day. Soon afterward, the dot-com bubble burst. There was a lot of blame. And overnight, in the boardrooms of companies from coast to coast, a word that had been the holy grail of the "new economy" became a word that could get you fired: *branding*.

There is irony too. Marketing departments were slashed, even closed altogether—just when companies with more competition than ever in shrinking markets needed them most.

One Small Detail: It Ain't Branding

Here's what they missed:

What they had been spending billions on and calling "branding" *wasn't branding*. It was entertaining. It was goofy names and logos. It was spending huge amounts to put cute words and pictures in the path of millions of consumers. Anything to get noticed. Anything to make a BANG!

But it had virtually nothing to do with creating real brands. Not the way the great Brand Titans who invented it meant branding. And today, in spite of all the lessons that should have been learned, seven out of ten companies still operate on the verge of brand oblivion epitomized by that disaster.

Yet the cure is nearly always waiting right under the nose of any company who looks for it, and then follows the simple and practical rules in the pages ahead.

Real Branding

This book is about removing the obstacles keeping "Johnny" and so many others from uncovering the Big Idea inside their brands.

That means it's about three things:

It's about thinking of brands in a surprisingly easy, everyday way that makes branding intuitive, demystifying the process of finding and expressing your big idea so that after you read about it, you can actually do it.

It's about transforming your business by putting your brand on a very focused kind of diet-and-fitness program—a super-effective regimen that will break the addiction to shallow, sugary conceits, melt the flab of puffy claims, and lean you down to the muscle that can make you a #1 brand.

And ultimately, it's about the fact that you really can create an entire turnaround for your strategy and position in about eight weeks—a workable, believable, #1 position in the minds of your targets—whether you're Ford Motors or Frankie's Lawn & Garden. In other words, it's about *real brands*—real brands versus the empty shells that are assets waiting to happen. Brands based on a real motivating difference that culminates in a *Dominant Selling Idea*—the big idea inside the message of every great, lasting brand. A real brand sets you up to be #1 in the specialty you choose. It grabs a place in the prospect's mind that no competitor can share, puts you on the short list for RFPs, and gives you a head start on every sale . . .

plus one more thing: *the internal by-product*. A real brand brings new energy to any company that acquires it, enabling everyone to focus and march in the same direction.

This is anything but marketing fluff. You'll find that it's applied sales physics. Take, for example, the seventh axiom in Chapter 4: "If you build a better mousetrap, *absolutely no one gives a s - - t.*" In fact, they secretly hate you for disrupting their impossible schedules with a new concept they have to learn about, decide if they can trust, and teach others to implement. No one ever sees what you see until you show them and sell them.

The only thing that can vault your brand over this firewall without a $50 million ad budget is the same as it was in the ancient time of Demosthenes—an idea—taken from a very special category of ideas. To be precise, a selling idea. We'll show you exactly why a selling idea is different from all other kinds of ideas and how to identify the one big idea for your brand in just forty working days.

The Sexiest Thing of All

Fear not. No one demands that you be dull. Creativity, color, and fun will always be the body of standout marketing and communication. But the heart is the selling idea. Idea first, entertainment second—or no real brand. Otherwise, your expensive advertising and brochures will be like a new sports car delivered without an engine—pretty, but with no means of driving itself into the mind of the customer. When you follow the simple advice in the pages ahead, you'll understand how to do the hardest, but most critical thing in marketing: make your *product the star*, not a sock puppet or a crowd of cats. Because in the end, the sexiest thing of all is increased sales.

Use Only as Directed

Please heed this advice: like any good self-improvement process, Part One is the crucial part, even though it's not the action plan or specific steps you might think of as the process itself. That comes in Part Two. Part One is where we figure out how much or how little we're really like "Johnny." We'll see the miscues and omissions that keep Johnny from finding his real #1 brand. And we'll get the rules and directions, laced with anecdotes and success stories we need to buy in, psych ourselves up, and take action. Because all coaches and psychologists know the most important phase of the program is . . . you ready . . . the mental one.

Not a new concept, we know, but it's 80 percent of this game, too. The eight-week positioning process succeeds more by adjusting how you think than any other factor. Bottom line: the "how-to" program at the end of this book is useless without understanding all the rules and principles that begin a few pages from now. They're the brains that move the muscle of your lean, real brand.

Found Money

What you will find at the end of this book is money. This is a guarantee. At the very least, found money in the form of better market awareness, better close ratios, and increased sales on your tight budget. At most, a transformation of your people and your business from the inside out: new vision, new purpose, new energy, new prospects, new products, and new asset value for the whole enterprise based on the galvanizing power of a Dominant Selling Idea. We've seen this transformation happen time and time again, and it can happen to you. It's the highest-markup, lowest-cost, asset-enhancing endeavor that any business can make because all it takes is a few weeks of focus and a few blank sheets of paper to write on. With a yield like that, who wouldn't try?

PART ONE

Thinking

1. Back to School

CHAPTER 1

So Why Can't Johnny Brand?

The last time I looked, the road to brand heaven didn't go through Harvard. In fact, they had a NO TRESPASSING sign.

Guru Mahatma Mahareshi "Mahesh" Goldberg

With everything on the line for today's companies, how can so many smart people in businesses big and small keep missing the boat with their brands?

Three Main Reasons

1. In the twenty-first century, believe it or not, what we're about to show you is still not taught in business schools.

If you have a Harvard, Stanford, or Wharton MBA, you know what we're talking about. Finance, accounting, and organizational theory are drilled into you all day long. But how and why you need a USP (*Unique Selling Proposition*)—which today we call a *Dominant Selling Idea*—is nowhere to be found. Academics must think that selling (capitalism) is crass or déclassé, because we've been polling graduates over the past ten years about how much practical branding they're taught and other than Marketing Management 101 and an occasional elective, the answer remains nada. This has to be why we've been to so many meetings where the discussion goes like this:

> MBA VENTURE CAPITALIST PARTNER:
> "We've hired a great new CEO, our third, and we like senior management. The burn rate is down to $100,000 per month. The technology is great, the product is out of beta and will be 'GA' in sixty days. The only question mark is we're not clear on the value proposition. We don't know if the market wants the product. Other than that, I'd say we're right on plan."

> FIVE OTHER MBA VCS (AROUND TABLE):
> (Heads nod).

We guarantee you, these people haven't been thinking about the brand. Some eventually learn by trial and error. Most go on like they always have, which is *your* golden opportunity.

2. *The tyranny of the Three Ts.*

Theories, Trendiness, and Totems are the Three Ts proffered by consultants, authors, and agencies trying to convince the needy that a *new*, proprietary panacea has been revealed that will float us to Brand Valhalla.

Tantalizing coinage like brand charisma, brand chronicles, brand karma, brand ethos, brand surprise, and brand warfare are the kind of thing we're talking about. These words describe what you get as a result after building a brand on a real, Dominant Selling Idea, as we'll see on the following pages. But taken alone, none of them are prescriptive of anything. When a consultant tells you, "The answer is brand charisma. $50,000, please," what do you exactly do?

Too much of the Three Ts leads directly to pseudo–brand-messaging tactics impelled by the same psychological charade. Here's a famous one:

"Sell the sizzle, not the steak."

This leads some companies to believe, in effect, that they can manufacture sizzle and actually forget about the steak. Have you ever gone to The Palm Steakhouse in New York City and ordered a twenty-four–ounce plate of *sizzle?* It is and always will be about the steak, my friends, when you're building a #1 brand. The steak is the vessel with the vitamins, the protein, the flavor, the color, the history, the process, the culture, and the complexity. Make your steak the idea and the star, and the sizzle will pop and snap better and louder than all the others, by default.

Too much theory, not enough reality, is an obstructive force that keeps Johnny and his good company from developing a good brand.

3. *But the biggest reason of all is* fear.

Branding and positioning require decisive commitment to a single path, and that means risk. The *positioning paradox* is that the power of your message is directly proportional to how simple you can make it and how few words and images you can use to say it. Amateurs are petrified not to list every possible feature and benefit in every communication, afraid they'll leave something on the table and miss some fraction of the market. But by saying everything, they heave themselves upon the clutter and end up saying nothing—too afraid to do the one thing that they must do: *choose.*

Professionals know branding is about relentless focus on the most singular message, always. They narrow the story all the way down to the big idea and its key associations to create a trim, lean, idea-centered brand. It takes some guts.

Taking the first step of any commitment is the hardest. If you're not sure about this, ask any skydiver. But once you commit, it's amazing how clarifying and empowering that step can be for an entire organization, let alone the marketplace.

Here's a direct challenge: If you have the discipline to follow the principles in this book, if you can trust your instruments in the clouds, as pilots say, to make the hard choices that all great marketers make, you'll be in a distinct minority in your industry—with the distinct advantage that comes from an unforgettable, idea-centered real selling brand.

If a Real Brand Is an Asset, What's It Worth in Dollars and Cents?

What's a strong brand worth in monetary terms? What should you invest? A whole subset of the branding industry has formed around the need for some execs to see a spreadsheet before they can justify spending—particularly for something as "soft" and subjective as brand development. The brand economics firms have dozens of benchmarks to measure "familiarity" and "favorability," in order to determine "brand health" versus competitors' in a category. They have data to support the claim that strong brands can contribute from 5 to 80 percent of the total market value of a corporation when total capitalized value is compared to asset value, for example. You can do this math on any company that has a real selling brand.

But in the spirit of common sense, let's ask it another way:

What's the value of a referral from an old friend versus a cold call?
What's the value of a doctor's reputation?
What's the value of having every employee on the same mission?
What's the value of a Dominant Selling Idea that can set you apart instantly from every other product in the industry—yet is so simple that every manager can repeat it, every salesperson can repeat it, every secretary, every analyst, every trade reporter, and every champion in the customer's organization can repeat it to peers?

The answer is *more*. More market share, more sales, more competitive strength, more growth, and more asset value for your company than you'd have without it. We've seen basic, redirected brand positioning based on an authentic Dominant Selling Idea increase sales from 10 to 100 percent. We've seen it transform companies inside and out with renewed energy and purpose. We've seen it determine success versus failure. In all cases, the average time to lay down the rails and get the train on the track is about forty business days. Used as directed, your commitment to this process is never wasted. Between the time investment for you and your staff, and the optional outsourcing of research, copyrighting, and design, we're talking about a cost in thousands. It can easily return millions.

Branding Anything

Finally, we have some good news and some *good* news.

The good news is that you can brand anything. By *anything*, we mean a product, a service, a religion, a nation, a holiday, a movie, a politician, an animal, a celebrity, or yourself if you're in the marketplace. If you ever doubt this, remind yourself that Frank Perdue branded a chicken. Perrier branded water. Florida branded sunshine. Size and wealth do not matter. Some of the biggest corporations with huge marketing budgets are adrift and in deadly default, while some of the tiniest have unique, idea-centered brands that set them apart brilliantly within their domains. You'll see plenty of specific examples when we practice the building blocks at the end of Part One.

Now for the *good* news—and we have to put this delicately: Based on twenty-five years of statistical analysis, you can be reasonably sure that your competition's branding . . . stinks. It's either non-existent, or it's based on internal conceits that have nothing to do with a selling idea or a differentiating value that the customer wants. In other words, most companies breathe their own fumes. For every ten companies, the average is one with a strong brand position, two that get credit for legitimate attempts, and seven that are awash in platitudes and puffery. Later, when you're attuned to the process, we want you to do your own survey by flipping through magazines and trade journals or clicking Web sites. Then call us at the house on the weekend if you discover that it's not seven out of ten.

There are a few notable exceptions to this standard. The great consumer packaged goods firms like Procter & Gamble and Masterfoods, whose products line the supermarket shelves, have lived and breathed brand science for nearly a century. They and their counterparts at great ad agencies uncovered many of the commandments we'll honor in the coming pages.

But for the vast majority, real branding eludes them. This is your great opportunity. You don't have to be a branding brain surgeon to make a big relative impact for yourself. You simply have to *do it* to separate yourself from the pack.

With one exception . . .

The One Caveat

To attempt this yourself, you have to have the Big Qualification. Don't worry. We think you have it or you wouldn't be reading this book. (We always wanted to say that.) The Big Qualification is not dramatic, but it's more important than everything else combined. You must, above all, have a genuine, honest love and enthusiasm for your product. This passion outweighs every other talent—and even if you've never created anything in your life, it provides you with at least one creative ticket to build at least one dominant brand, *your own*. Doing the branding for other people's products—as consultants and agencies do, day in and day out—takes deeper professional training and skill that comes from a long-term commitment to the trade. But all the principles and methods are exactly the same.

If you're not sure you have the Big Qualification, our advice is: read the book anyway. Then, using its principles, give the branding process a try. If you can't find your potential #1 brand position in eight weeks, in spite of what "established" consultants may tell you, it can't be done. Your problem is more serious than your strategy. Either fix the product, get another product, or get another job. Life is too short to toil for a product or company that's unworthy of your passion, talent, and love.

Three Days from Now at 8 A.M. . . .

On the morning of Day 4, at normal reading speed, you can easily have finished this book. You'll know what the experts know. It'll be Day 1 of the rest of your brand life. If you jump on it, you can only go forward and eventually you can reach this goal—to own a real selling brand that makes you #1 in your target customers' mind.

CHAPTER 2

Quick—What's a Brand? (The Chemistry of One-Track Minds)

If you're in business, you're a brand in the customer's mind. It's not optional. It's a fact of life. So shape it yourself, or competitors and customers will assign a brand for you—and, I promise, you won't like the tag line.

Guru Mahatma Mahareshi "Mahesh" Goldberg

Your Single-Minded Urge

You walk into a party. There's a woman in a police uniform, a young man with blue spiked hair, and three other people in casual clothes. Okay, that's a lady cop and a punky teenager who's probably on drugs. Who are the other three? The hostess comes over. "Let me introduce you to Dr. Harwood, head of neurosurgery; Bill Clendenen, the attorney who just got another Kennedy off the hook; and my friend, Bob." You slot Bob as an accountant. Then you see his Patek Philippe. Bob moves up to investment banker. Between the uniforms, your hostess and your preconceptions, you've just judged, valued, categorized, and labeled (i.e., you've positioned and branded) six people in sixty seconds. And guess what, they've just branded you.

We don't think about it; we just do it. It's an instinctive habit we've gained over the past ten million years to mentally package the chaos of information all around us, then format it to fit in neat spaces in the brain for instant retrieval at a party, at the supermarket, or on the battlefield—a single-minded urge to simplify.

So . . . What's a Real Brand?

Nike shoes, Burger King, and Colgate Toothpaste are.

So are France, Italy, O. J. Simpson, Abraham Lincoln, lawyers, plumbers, James Bond movies, Little League baseball, Batman, Superman, Christianity, Judaism, Harvard, Notre Dame, the Beatles, the Royal Family, Greenpeace, Green Giant, NBA, and NRA—not to mention the sound of a violin versus the sound of a country banjo. Close your eyes, picture the American flag, and free associate for three seconds. Now do the Nazi flag.

Real brands are an amazingly efficient mental magic trick where a few words, a symbol, or even a sound triggers an instant snapshot that's totally distinguishable from a million others residing in our heads—one composite photo distilled from every message, touch, and experience we've ever had with the item in question. We have an unlimited capacity to file such brands in our trillion-neuron brains. They simply have to fit the right format for entry, storage, and retrieval.

Nothing says you have to be a commercial product to function as a real brand in the collective mind. You just need two requirements, both simple and profound: You need an *exclusive name* that's attached to an *exclusive idea of value*—the more believable and emotional, the better.

Good Brand Versus Bad Brand— a Practical Definition

Did you ever hear the wise old saying, "The opposite of love isn't hate; it's apathy." It's the same with brands. A good brand versus a bad brand isn't a brand you love versus a brand you hate. It's not the Union Army versus the Confederacy. Both of those were great real brands with specific, emotional power.

The opposite of a good brand is a meaningless, undifferentiated brand—an empty brand shell without idea or substance. A weak and ineffective brand. That's what we're fighting against every day of our brand lives.

A Real Selling Brand

Now here's the ultimate brand judgment: if commercial success is our goal, we must enable our real brand to be a *real selling brand*. A brand with a value so unique and superior, it's the #1 value in its class. All this means is that your brand's big idea must be a very specific kind of idea—a Dominant Selling Idea. An idea that fuses your name with an idea of unique, superlative value. That's it. Your path to glory. We'll be explaining the concept in detail over the next few chapters.

Finally (This Is Important), Let's Get Straight on the Word "Branding"

We're down to the meaning of that little *ing* that turns *brand* into an active verb for businesspeople, professors, nuns, televangelists, and Johnny himself—all of whom invariably get it wrong, leading to the kind of trivializing that causes their brand trouble in the first place. Too many folks think "branding" is what airlines do when they repaint the planes every few years, or what banks do when they refresh all the signage in their lobbies and reengineer their logos. In the airlines' case, they spend millions to update the image on the tails of their airplanes. Then they arrive late, stick you in a cramped seat with your knees bumping the food tray, charge you $1,000 more than the guy sitting next to you because you committed the crime of not including a Saturday night stay, and lose your %$##@%!!! luggage! The experience, value impression, and relative position in the passenger's mind remain exactly the same.

Friends, this is not branding in our terms. This is paint on the surface of branding. Branding is about finding a specific IDEA that you stand for, finding a way to own that idea in a credible way, and ultimately building total trust that you will always deliver. It's about your walk—well before your talk. You make physical, material adjustments to your product, service, and market conduct as necessary to align with that idea. Then you tell the world. And then, if you want to repaint the planes, be our guest.

Even in the world of theater, what actors say is less important than what they do. That's why any director will tell you, "Action is character." In our world, action is branding.

In the Time Before Cocoa Puffs

Our single-minded drive to brand things wasn't created by consultants. It was created a million years ago so that humans could survive in the jungle. Branding served evolution by predicting instantly whom you could trust versus who would shrink your head. It took the guesswork out of that Tyrannosaurus rex sleeping next to the lava pool. You didn't have to get out of your tree and poke him with a stick to remember, "Oh yeah, flight." The flip side of our natural urge to brand is to want things branded. That's why we respond so well when smart companies make it easy by furnishing us with a quality, credible brand construct. It's how we're wired. And if companies don't provide it, guess what—*we brand them anyway*, just like we judge and brand people, on our own terms and often at their peril. These are the branding facts of life in business and in everyday living. Only a fool or short-sighted company would try to duck this reality or, just as dangerously, try to brand while ignoring the few precious rules of great brands that come straight from human nature itself, making them timeless and unchangeable, as we'll see.

At a conference recently, we actually overheard a business pundit telling a CEO, "Branding is out." He might as well have said, "The human psyche is out." What he meant was that companies realize that spending large sums to inflate weak

13

products ends up nowhere. He meant puffery is out, but he mistakenly called it branding. Maybe a highly paid consultant can afford to be confused. But you can't afford to waste your rightful asset in markets as brutally competitive as they are now. We promise from now on, you won't.

To Be or Not to Be—That's Not the Question

And so, by the simple act of opening your doors for business, as a law firm or a taco stand, you become a brand in the eyes of everyone who sees you, touches you, or buys from you. The only choice you have is to become either a negative, undifferentiated brand or a powerful, motivating, and dominant one—a real selling brand. A momentous choice that any company can make *no matter what your size or resources*. Smart companies treat the choice like a parental responsibility. They know they can't "slap a brand" onto their business. It's in the DNA—a true tangible asset. It's how they connect to an even more valuable asset—disk space in the brains of their target customers.

Now let's check the fundamentals for #1 brands.

CHAPTER 3

The Rules for #1 Brands

At Wimbledon, the number one player pauses before the final match to huddle with his famous coach. Tennis fans around the world would give anything to hear the secret advice whispered into the ear of the world's greatest player. What the coach tells him is "Bend your knees."

Guru Mahatma Mahareshi "Mahesh" Goldberg

"Wisdom for Dummies"

The best people in any endeavor are distinguished in an important way. They have exceptional mastery of the fundamentals. It's true in sports, art, music, science, succeeding on a diet, and branding.

In our case, the fundamentals are bits and pieces of psychological wisdom—wisdom about what people want, what makes them care, what makes them not just notice but remember, and, ultimately, what makes them choose.

The wonderful part is, neither you nor we have to discover these fundamentals on our own, any more than we need to invent the Ten Commandments. They're waiting for anyone who asks. And their main requirement isn't talent. It's humility. Humility lets us absorb common sense and embrace the fact that what's in the customer's mind is far more important than what's in our mind—no matter how smart we think we are. You can test yourself: If the word *"Dummies"* up there offends you personally because your intellect is actually high, you need more humility.

The Brand Titans

Our spiritual forefathers had a creative hot streak when they wrote all the bibles that still guide civilizations two thousand years later. Our branding forefathers had a golden period too. It lasted from about 1923 to 1965, when the last truly great marketing book was written. A few have been worthy of honorable mention since, but none have reached founding-father status like Claude C. Hopkins, Victor O. Schwab, John Caples, David Ogilvy, and Rosser Reeves.

To the Brand Titans, the drab hallways of the early mail order advertising firms and Madison Avenue agencies were like the dusty streets of Jerusalem and Mecca to the writers of the holy books. It was the cradle of "branding-ization." Like most originals, they were ahead of their time, mining the science from a field that was considered, at best, a questionable art, and writing it down in brief but practical books that mirrored the clarity and simplicity of their principles.

Our first ad agency jobs in New York put us under the wing of people who were disciples and actually knew some of these men. Their books are now mostly out of print and their anecdotes are antiquated, but their big ideas about big ideas are timeless.

What They Found—the Granite Pages

We're about to unveil the Granite Pages—the fundamental rules uncovered by the Brand Titans, filtered and distilled by our twenty-five years of trial and error. They are the nutritional basis of all #1 brands, the keys to cutting the fat, trimming your brand to its irreducible meaning, then building lean brand muscle for the rest of your life. Keep them in front of you from now on. They're called the Granite Pages because they would have been chiseled in stone if it weren't for the shipping costs.

Granite Pages I –VI: Rules to Differentiate and Define

Granite Page I is the largest because it's the mother of them all.

GRANITE PAGE I

The Number 1 Is Holy

IN the world of real selling brands, the number 1 and its properties hold all the answers. Because if falling in love with a digit is possible, humans have an abiding affair with the number one. The remaining two zillion might just as well be math.

We're fascinated by and we remember who comes in first—the first man on the moon, the winner of the Kentucky Derby, the first man to climb Mount Everest, Olympic Gold Medal winners—but almost none that follow. We reward #1 out of all proportion. The winners of a golf tournament by a stroke or a marathon by a millisecond aren't twice as good as the losers—but we give them more prize money than all the other contestants combined plus all the endorsements. We can't remember who came in next even when we try. Take the five Miss America finalists out there on stage. Five big smiles. Five fluttering hearts. Boom. Down drops the diamond tiara. Winner: *idolized*. Runners-up: *vaporized*.

It follows that we have one god, we seek to be "at one" with ourselves, we have one spouse, one president, and one favorite Chinese restaurant, not necessarily in that order. Our entire cultural and philosophical system is built on being #1 in some area or specialty if we want to be famous, important, and influential. Naturally, so must your brand.

In everyday terms, *positioning*, the common branding word, is simply your specialty—the ability, action, or attribute you offer that others don't. It's what people seek to buy from *you* because it's your focus and they think you do it best. In our process, we replace the word *positioning* with *specialty* because it forces us to think about differentiating ourselves in the sharpest, most specific, most superlative way. It points us to the only difference that matters—the one that tips customers in your direction versus all others at the deciding moment. As we'll see, such a difference is born not merely by having a specialty, but a *specialty that you are #1 in.*

But what if right now you're not considered #1 in some specialty? What if your brand seems so far from #1 you can't imagine how you'll ever get there? Do not—we repeat DO NOT seek a refund for the price of this book. Read "The Five Rules of One" that follow and you'll see not only how the first Granite Page works, but why your opportunities to claim #1 status are unlimited.

The Five Rules of One

1. The "One Item of 'Carry-On'" Rule

When seeking to differentiate your brand, no matter how much information you offer, when you've finished pitching:

People only remember one thing.

So when you feel that irresistible, amateur force moving you to list every product feature in every brand message—get over it. It's not that we don't have the brain capacity, it's that we also have a brain reflex that synthesizes details, images, and feelings on any subject into single thought packages for easy storage and retrieval from our mental "overhead bin." You can give people long lists of features and benefits. But when they walk away, their minds morph it down to that one piece of mental "carry-on." A key corollary is that this salient idea, once carried aboard, preempts all others and will stubbornly remain in place, virtually forever, until a more compelling idea physically dislodges it.

A reporter once asked a woman what a senate candidate had said in a campaign speech. The candidate spoke passionately for nearly an hour covering every point of his platform. "What did he say?" the man asked. She replied, "He was against taxes."

Here's another classic. The O. J. Simpson prosecution spent nine months and millions of dollars laying out a case that was so scientifically detailed, so obsessively logical that no rational group of people could possibly fail to convict on the weight of the evidence. Except the jury. For them, it all became a blur, erased by "the one thing to remember" defense lawyer Johnny Cochran shrewdly suggested on day 1: You can retain ten thousand bits of evidence, or save the trouble and just retain this: *O.J. was framed by racist cops.* Cochran even provided a famous tag line to make it even more convenient. "If the glove doesn't fit, you must acquit." The jury "carried on" the one item it chose to remember, and left ten thousand valuable bits of information at the curb with the skycap, minus a tip.

2. The "Dominant Selling Idea" Rule
Naturally, the single item of "carry-on" that people choose is the one they deem most precious. Likewise, if your brand is to

have one paramount idea with the best chance of being installed in the brain, that idea must fuse your name to a specialty that's the most *superlative, important, believable, memorable,* and *tangible* you can find. A specialty with the Five Selling Ingredients. To be specific:

1. *Superlative.* It must promise me something nobody else does, signaling you're #1 in whatever you do, the best at something.
2. *Important.* What you're #1 in has to be something that matters—something I really want or would be in the market for if I knew about it.
3. *Believable.* There has to be a unique, plausible reason why you claim the above that makes logical sense.

Only a specialty with these first three ingredients gets you across the moat and into the castle. Then, if you want to stick there, your specialty and everything surrounding it must be made:

4. *Memorable.* It has to link to an emotional feeling—the humanizing factor that gives it penetrating power. Finally and most importantly, it has to be
5. *Tangible.* It must perform in a way that's totally aligned and consistent with all your claims—the ultimate test. If not, no matter how lean, strong, and appealing you are, you'll be mounted on the catapult in two seconds and shot back over the wall without a net.

A specialty with all five ingredients is positioning incarnate, designed to motivate as much as it differentiates.

When such a specialty is attached to your name, it's called a *Dominant Selling Idea (DSI),* something we'll cover in great detail in Section II. With a DSI, your target can't even think your name without automatically linking it to an idea of superior value that sets you apart as #1 in your specialty. And, just as sweet, the target can't think of that specialty either, without thinking your name first.

If the #1 spot you want is already taken by a competitor, *go to Rule 3.*

3. The "Unlimited Specialty" Rule

There's this big, lucky paradox that makes it possible for any-one to succeed at finding their #1 brand idea, even though it may seem that opportunities to be #1 are, by definition, lim-ited. The paradox is this: Yes, under the Rules of One, people focus on just one #1 brand in any perceived business specialty, but people can remember an unlimited number of specialties and categories!

Think about the thousands upon thousands of individual sub-jects you can instantly recall from sports to food to favorite songs to movie stars. You can articulate rich, specific impressions of your favorite in every specialty. Indeed, you can discuss sec-ondary and tertiary players too at times—but a cogent impres-sion of your #1 is guaranteed. Keep in mind then that even though there is only one Olympic Gold Medal to be won in each event, there will always be hundreds of events—*specialties*—to be the winner of! And when in doubt, we can always invent more specialties or even more categories because of . . .

4. The "Captain Kirk" Rule

In the second *Star Trek* movie, when a young lieutenant de-spaired about an impossible dilemma, Bones spoke wistfully about Captain Kirk's legendary out-of-the-box thinking. It had gotten him through all eighty episodes and would presumably do so today. Kirk was the only cadet at Captain school who ever solved the *Kobayashi Maru*, the great unsolvable riddle in the final exam. Since there was no possible solution within the lim-its of the rules, Kirk reprogrammed the computer to change the rules.

This has big implications for the way we brand. When we

look at our market and see that a competitor is way ahead in the game, we don't despair. The quickest path to #1 is to change the rules that define your specialty, then claim the gold medal in the new one. In other words, when you're not #1 in your specialty, create another specialty to be #1 in.

Combining two established specialties to form a third illustrates one of several basic ways we're going to show you how to do this. Let's say there is an athlete who's clearly #1 at cross-country skiing. You're a good cross-country skier but you can also target shoot. You create a new event called the cross-country ski & target shoot, better known as the Olympic Biathlon. Now you can declare yourself first in the Biathlon. Subaru had an all-wheel–drive station wagon in a world of expensive, gas-guzzling SUV trucks. They knew there was a market for vehicles that combined the best of both at a moderate price. Subaru designated itself the *SUV Wagon*. And suddenly, in this new specialty, Subaru was, and still is, #1.

5. The "Eye of the Beholder" Rule

The last Rule of One pertains to #1 status itself. Even though what's in the customer's mind is what ultimately defines brand meaning and value, as designers of the brand, we have great influence over what gets chosen as that one item of mental "carry-on." Because the secret to all this is:

#1 is what we say it is.

The definition of #1 in a specialty can be whatever we determine it to be, so long as it's believable and we perform as claimed.

The traditional definition of #1 as biggest sales volume or highest revenue is just one version of #1. In reality, #1 has as many guises as there are key attributes and measures or differences the market can legitimately value. Microsoft is the #1 giant software company in the world. But there are a hundred other software specialties with a #1 brand in every one. Norton is the leader in antivirus software. Quicken is the leader in personal finance software. Oracle is the leader in database software. *The only #1 that matters is to be #1 in the minds of our customers.*

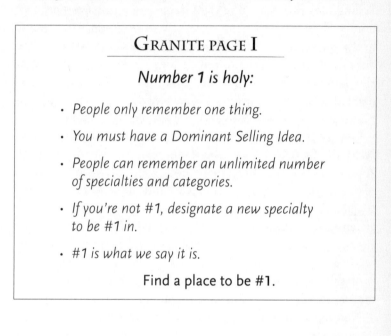

Granite page I

Number 1 is holy:

- *People only remember one thing.*

- *You must have a Dominant Selling Idea.*

- *People can remember an unlimited number of specialties and categories.*

- *If you're not #1, designate a new specialty to be #1 in.*

- *#1 is what we say it is.*

Find a place to be #1.

Granite page II

Your Name

The sweetest word in the universe is your own name. The sweetest word in the brand universe is your brand's name.

A ROSE by any other name would be a Schnitzel Weed. Can you imagine giving your sweetie a dozen long-stemmed Schnitzel Weeds for Valentine's Day? Pretty as it is, do you think a Schnitzel Weed would have become the symbol of romance?

We are programmed to think and organize by name, starting with our own, the first word we learn. When we think about a brand, the thought starts at its name. Names are special words that hold concentrated magic. In a real brand, if the Dominant Selling Idea is protein, the right name is your first essential vitamin. The very best names are easy to pronounce, appealing to the ear, sticky to the memory and whenever possible, link us directly to the Dominant Selling Idea so that the name literally launches your DSI every time, no further explanation needed. That means every utterance of such a name is a complete, mini–selling-unit in and of itself. Pretty efficient.

One of our favorite examples was in a recent story in *The New York Times*. It was about an obscure fish from South America called the Patagonian Tooth Fish. It was delicious and plentiful, but the market for it was nil because nobody wanted to eat a Patagonian Tooth Fish, let alone see one. Until someone renamed it *Chilean Sea Bass*. The rest is food service history. By the same token, if Ralphie Lipschitz's mother had known he wanted to grow up to be a world-famous clothing designer, she probably could have called him Ralph Lauren right off the bat and saved him the trouble of changing his name years later.

Naming is fun and rewarding, easy to practice and we'll cover it step by step—including how to know when it's time to change yours—in Chapter 8. For now, remember:

GRANITE PAGE II
Your name:

The right name is your most powerful single tool.

The Universal Paradox

The narrower you focus, the wider your message goes.

IN branding, the more features you show, the less you are seen. The more details you provide, the more vaguely you communicate. The more directions you give, the harder it is to be located. The higher the number, the lower the value.

Now that sounds like a guru talking, doesn't it?

This is called the *Positioning Paradox* and it stems, of course, from the Rules of One. By capturing undisputed leadership in a single important benefit, you are most likely to be noticed, remembered, and associated with a series of other great benefits, made all the more credible because you have reached prominence in one meaningful specialty.

It's the bed-of-nails phenomenon in reverse. A bed with a single nail sticking up will penetrate you the second you lie down. But a thousand nails can't penetrate anything. The pressure of each nail is completely diffused by all the others around it.

The Universal Paradox is also behind the *Least Number of Words* principle for Dominant Selling Ideas. Generally, the shorter and crisper the length, the more impact to the DSI:

ADP—*the payroll company*
Rolex—*the luxury watch*
Duracell—*the longest-lasting battery*
ESPN—*the sports channel*

Owning the gold medal in one critical value like safety or durability associates you with a ream of other important benefits for your target: quality of construction, intelligent engineering, company caring, trust, and on and on.

It takes discipline and, frankly, some guts for businesses to thwart their instinct to tell all in every communication. But professionals know:

GRANITE PAGE III

The Universal Paradox:

In every aspect of branding, you say the most by saying the least. The simplest message wins.

GRANITE PAGE IV

Own It

IT'S not enough to be technically superlative. You have to *appear* superlative by becoming sole owner of one particular difference in the customer's mind. The biggest lesson of the famous self-help book *Everything I Ever Needed to Know I Learned in Kindergarten* ends right here.

We don't share.

As a famous entrepreneur once said, "I can tell you the most important rule for business success in two words, five letters: *Own it!*" The owner always gets the lion's share of control, money, and fame.

This holds for brands, too. The process is simple: you're awarded ownership of a superlative difference when you're *first to be perceived* as the one who can, does, or will do something *best*.

If in fact you are the only one in the world who does it, that's great, but you don't have to be. Because once you've established "owner" status, it tends to stick stubbornly in people's heads, even when others arrive with the same attributes—as long as you keep proclaiming and performing.

Exactly *how* we achieve ownership status is merely the subject of the next two hundred pages of this book. We'll get there. For now, just remember . . .

GRANITE PAGE IV

2 words, 5 letters:

Own it.

🏛 GRANITE PAGE V 🏛

The Importance of Being Important

THE unique promise put forth in your Dominant Selling Idea has to matter more to your prospect than any other promise you or your competitors can make for it to be either dominant or a selling idea. It has to have a direct, obvious impact on either pain or desire. As simple as it may sound, customers have to want it. Massive numbers of Harvard and Stanford MBAs lost billions of dollars of investor capital by ignoring this Granite Page, which is also the second ingredient for a Dominant Selling Idea. They built dot-com businesses around concepts that were brilliant in every respect except one: people didn't want the product. In other words, the idea wasn't important to the prospect.

So you may proclaim to the world that your store has the world's largest selection of brown ties. But if prospects don't care about brown ties, you'll need another DSI.

GRANITE PAGE V

Importance:

Choose the most obvious need, the most powerful want.
Your difference must *matter*.

GRANITE PAGE VI

Credibility

A SELLING idea is a promise of value. A Dominant Selling Idea is a promise of value that is not only superlative and important, it must be *believable* in two ways or the prospect's mind will slam shut so fast you'll bang your nose on the gate.

The prospect has to believe, first of all, that your implied promise can be logically true and believe, second of all, that you are qualified to deliver on it.

Today more than ever, your prospect's bulls--t antenna is fully extended at all times. Nobody has the money, the time, or the patience to be burned these days. Before they'll admit your proposition to the brain for consideration, prospects subject every claim to two immediate tests: (1) Is the claim plausible? (2) Is it plausible coming from *you*? If the answer to either is no, you're dead.

Question 2 is important because it's flouted daily by so many large companies who should know better. They think that just because their brand represents a symbol of quality in one specialty, slapping their name on any other specialty will automatically draw buyers like a magnet. Wrong. At the moment of truth—the moment of any purchase decision— nobody hands their money to someone they don't think of as the *most qualified* in that specialty, any more than they'd ask the world's best attorney to do their heart transplant the day after he'd gotten them acquitted for a capital crime. They'd thank him for the offer and call a heart surgeon. It's the double-edged sword of having a great, strong brand. The more powerfully you're identified with one particular specialty, the more challenging it can be to be credible in others. Actors call it being typecast.

The exception is when you extend yourself into an area that seems reasonably related to your present one. Nike's expertise in shoe technology can plausibly transfer to socks or laces or even sportswear. But Nike's on more dangerous ground when it tries to put its brand on a portable CD player. For that, most people will still think of Sony. Ferrari engineers the speediest Italian sports cars. But don't give me a Ferrari laptop for speedy computing. Give me a Dell with Intel inside.

Levi's understood this perfectly. No jeans brand was ever more famous or more experienced at making pants than Levi's. But when it was time to introduce a line of slacks for the growing business-casual market, they resisted the urge to call it Levi Khakis. They created a successful new brand called Dockers.

Toyota got it right when they wanted to introduce a new line of expensive cars in the United States. This world leader in moderately priced cars could have been forgiven for thinking a high-priced model would be a plausible brand extension. But they didn't. They knew their name would never stand for luxury. So they introduced a car named Lexus.

But Volkswagen, another multibillion-dollar company (means "people's car") sadly, didn't get it. They tried to introduce the Phaeton recently—a superluxury car with a big, shiny Volkswagen emblem on it. The car *is* absolutely stunning. We've seen it. And nobody will buy it because, when you finally have $60,000 in your hands and you can choose to have your snobby neighbors see you driving around town in a BMW, a Mercedes, or a Jag, you don't buy a Volkswagen. The Phaeton officially flopped in less than a year on the market, costing Volkswagen a bundle.

So don't assume your credibility automatically travels well. But don't take that as a bad thing, either. Enjoy the privileges of #1 status in the category or specialty you're in. Extend your line with utmost care and only to specialties that relate plausibly to your own. And choose a separate brand with a new name, new specialty, and new DSI when you wish to go beyond it.

For Every DSI, a Reason Why

The Brand Titans understood early on that people decide to buy for emotional reasons—then require an intellectual "reason why" to act on it. The reason why in effect gives the prospect "permission to believe"—a crucial part of the selling process. You could even call it "plausible buyability."

Ernie Boch was by far the most successful car dealer in Boston. His competitors all shouted about great service, great selection, and honest deals. But Ernie had a reason why that made prospects nod their heads. Ernie said over and over, "Ah prices ah lowah, because our costs ah lowah! We pay no finance chahges on ah cahs like otha dealahs. We buy ah cahs fa cash, so we can save you cash." People who were raised not to believe car dealers could believe Ernie Boch.

Snickers was just another candy bar until the Ted Bates Agency added a reason to believe it was OK to eat without feeling guilty. Snickers was "packed with high-protein peanuts to really satisfy" your hunger. Suddenly, a candy bar was a nutritious snack. Snickers gave people permission to buy. Sales jumped solely on the strength of a Dominant Selling Idea with a credible reason why:

Packed with peanuts, Snickers really satisfies!

GRANITE PAGE VI

Credibility:

Be believable or be erased.

CHAPTER 4

Granite Pages VII–XVII:
Rules to Penetrate and Stick

I had a point to make about memorability, but I forgot what I was going to say.

Guru Mahatma Mahareshi "Mahesh" Goldberg

With his usual eloquence, weaving a disarmingly simple yet brilliant parable, the Guru makes his point that a Dominant Selling Idea isn't much good if you can't remember it.

For your brand idea to perform as a selling idea, it has to penetrate the heads of customers. Then it has to stay there, and keep working long enough for the target to get to the mall. The Granite Pages now turn to the fundamentals that go hand in glove with differentiation—the enablers of penetration and memorability that attach to your idea and help install it in the minds of your prospects.

Granite page VII

The Mouse Trap

EVERY one of us in business, from the CEO on down, loves to breathe our own fumes. We spend every day immersed in our product, passionate about what we're creating, positive about its value, and, like a proud mother, convincing ourselves that anyone who even glimpses our little darling will see all the beauty and brilliance that we do. In short, we believe that since we've built a better mousetrap, the world will beat a path to our door.

Now let's get real.

No busy, overstressed, fire-putting-out, content-with-the-product-they-have-now person really wants to hear from you. Even when you do build a better mousetrap, the world thinks you're a giant pain in the ass.

Nobody has time, nobody has the patience, nobody wants to take the risk that your claims are exaggerated, nobody cares about your success, nobody wants to go through the political rigmarole of selling you into their organization. People don't like change and they don't want to switch. This is the reinforced door that stands between us and delivery of our Dominant Selling Idea. It only opens from the inside. We have to be invited in or we never get to tell our tale. What we say differentiates us. How we say it gets us inside. This is the humble reality we need to assume, embrace, and work under to achieve our #1 brand.

GRANITE PAGE VII

There is organized, armed resistance
to your better product.
It should humble you for the next ten Granite Pages.

GRANITE PAGE VIII

Make Me an Offer I Can't Refuse

YOUR brand must weave an offer into the pattern of its fabric, an *immediate* proposition that says, "There's a reasonable chance I will make your life 51 percent better if you listen to my message." *Fifty-one percent better* means that your proposition's value will overcome its costs, which include all the baggage you start with in Granite Page VII above. It will be worth my time, my risk, my inconvenience, my natural inertia, and my trauma from past bad buying decisions—not to mention my money.

To this day, there are eight human appeals that affect us all, and you must communicate at least one of them to your prospects immediately, directly, and unambiguously. Every person wants to be

Happier
Smarter
Healthier
Richer
Safer
More secure
More attractive
More successful

The value of these appeals may seem rather obvious when you look at them—but when we examine and rate some actual brands in the chapter on Dominant Selling Ideas, you'll be surprised at how much core brand messaging for even the largest companies contains not one of the eight in plain sight.

Your appeal has to be direct, powerful, and, above all, fast. As Renee Zellweger says to Tom Cruise in the film *Jerry McGuire* after his big declaration of love speech: "Stop! You had me at 'hello.'" Your appeal has to get your target at "hello" or the deadbolt goes on the door.

This requirement is literally illustrated during middle-of-family dinner telemarketing calls. From job hell, these poor souls have been stupidly instructed to engage the victim with a pleasantry to "warm 'em up." "Hello, Mr. Shinley? . . . Uhh, Mr. Sibley? How you doin' today?" Considering that they just jerked me up from the dinner table and, in my absence, three teenagers have just finished all the risotto before I got any, I say "Rotten!" and hang up.

But sometimes I feel pity. So I give the caller a friendly tip: "You have to understand, Amber, that I'm starting off angry, resistant, and negative toward you. You have only one chance to avoid a slam down. You have to open with an appealing offer so fast, I can't react any other way but to say, 'What is it?' Try this and don't even pause for breath or it's too late."

"Sir, if I could save you 50 percent on your phone bill and you wouldn't even have to switch carriers, you'd want to know about it, right?"

My attitude would then transform from pure annoyance to "This person may have something I want."

We must approach our target markets and craft our core message from that same humble position—offer and appeal first, small talk later.

GRANITE PAGE VIII

Appeal to me with an offer and put it out front.

⚏ GRANITE PAGE IX ⚏

Nobody Volunteers for Pain

FOR consumers, pain and distress occur in many forms—fear of a bad buying decision, inconvenience, frustration, confusion, overpayment, wasted time, anger that the old status quo was better than the new one, the stress of overcoming natural inertia, and on and on. All of these suck up precious time and energy and cause pain.

When there is even a hint that net pleasure may not supercede the prospect of pain, customers do not volunteer. You never even see them. They just turn and walk the other way.

This is why your message must be simple to understand, obvious in utility, risk-free, and appealing to a definite personal need. You must make your product look and be painless to buy.

Internet marketers like Amazon knew they were losing a large percentage of sales because of the cumbersome online ordering process. Customers would get through navigating the site, finding the book, preceding to checkout—then face twenty daunting questions in order to pay with a credit card, usually ending up with a series of error messages. Too many customers quit in frustration, vowing never to come back. In the minds of these customers, the Amazon brand meant *books online plus anger.*

Amazon acted to make it easier to buy, creating a "one-touch" ordering technology so customers could opt to enter their information once—then check out with a single click from then on. Amazon strengthened its brand by removing pain from the buying process, increasing sales as a result.

GRANITE PAGE IX

Take the pain out of the process.

GRANITE PAGE X

People Like What They Understand

THERE is no stronger psychological drive than a person's need to be understood and the corresponding need to understand. That's why moments of sudden realization are some of the most dramatic and inspiring that people can experience— the "Ah-hah! moment." People like what they understand and remember what they like.

The reverse has deadly opposite associations—fear of the unknown, failure, anxiety caused by confusion, and intolerance based on ignorance. Worse, there is no chance of creating trust without understanding. You don't want these kinds of associations within five hundred miles of your brand.

Quicken financial software sales were going up, but the rate of new buyers becoming "active" was actually slowing. Quicken found to their amazement that nearly 40 percent of the software packages that were purchased and carried home were never taken out of their shrink wrap! Buyers admitted that even though they bought it for all its new features, they dreaded the idea of starting it, not understanding it, and going through the pain of feeling stupid—even though they knew it was something they should do. It was Quicken's wake-up call to get back to its roots as the brand that's so simple to use, all you need to know is how to use a checkbook.

Work tirelessly to make your message simple and effortless. That goes for your products, too. In this age of overcomplication and burdensome, unnecessary choice posing as a benefit—the more quickly customers "get it," the more customers you'll have.

GRANITE PAGE X

People like what they understand, and they like the person who makes them understand it!

Make it simple to understand.

GRANITE PAGE XI

People Remember What They Feel

WHY do you think you remember exactly where you were and what you were doing during world-changing events in your life? September 11, 2001? The moment you proposed to your spouse? The time you broke your arm? The day the Red Sox lost the 1986 World Series? The moment Publisher's Clearing House showed up at your door with the $1,000,000 check, but they had the wrong house?

The reason is that the power, clarity, and endurance of memory is directly proportional to the amount of emotion attached to it. Emotion is the fuel that powers memory. And in the real brand world, powerful emotions can operate in much subtler forms than you'd think. The mistake is thinking that brand emotion emanates only from the big, obvious fireworks like love, sex, and fast cars. Every selling idea and buying decision can have an effective emotional component as long as it's based on the Eight Human Appeals. That means that at the purchase moment for even the most technical, back-office software at a bank, the buyer responds emotionally to the prospect of succeeding in his job, being more secure, feeling more important and understood—and the corresponding pain that would come from screwing up.

Watch a woman choosing between brands of dandruff shampoo in the supermarket aisle the night before a date. She's hypnotized, imagining the effect on her attractiveness, self-image, confidence, and romantic prospects by using one versus the other. This is a small, mundane, yet entirely emotional decision.

It goes without saying that emotion must be dyed into the wool of your Dominant Selling Idea. Emotion is generated to some degree just by our being #1. It is also generated by our level of "importance" to the customer. But it can really be boosted by the use of emotionally charged images or word metaphors to tap into the consumer's psyche.

Not always, mind you. That engineer buying the bank software gets hot and excited by hearing the term *robust platform architecture* and then seeing the numbers. But a life insurance customer needs that added metaphor that makes the DSI emotional and memorable. She needs to hear you're "the Good Hands People." If she's buying dinner rolls or snow tires, she responds similarly to the Pillsbury Doughboy and the baby sitting inside the Michelin.

As we said earlier, people need an intellectual "reason why" that establishes believability and "permission" to close the sale.

But the old adage is true. Emotion does the heavy lifting. It drives the feelings and the memory without which there would be no brand or the selling opportunities that go with it.

GRANITE PAGE XI

Emotion puts memory in motion.

𝕀 GRANITE PAGE XII 𝕀

To the Consistent Go the Spoils

CONSISTENCY may be "the hobgoblin of small minds," but it's the concrete in the foundation of every #1 brand. You put all your wood behind your arrow, in this case your Dominant Selling Idea, if you want maximum power at impact. And then you want to keep impacting. When your emotional component is inherently low—auto insurance versus auto racing, for example—consistency over time delivers the impact you need over time. "Little Brother Poking Torture" is a perfect example. This occurs when your big brother pokes you lightly over and over in the exact same spot and won't stop. At first it doesn't hurt. Then it's annoying. But pretty soon it's excruciating and you've actually got a bruise. The key is the *exact same spot*. If he'd poked you lightly all over, it'd be annoying but not effective.

Every brand component, message, and touch point must be consistent with your Dominant Selling Idea to achieve ownership, awareness, impact, and dominance itself. We call it *TCA (Total Consistent Alignment)*. Like every successful process, practice makes perfect. Maintaining consistency—poking in the same spot—is a daily requirement in the life of every #1 brand.

Done right, consistency is actually fun. Restaurants are particularly great at this. We walked into a rock-'n'-roll diner last week. There were guitars and hot rod parts all over the walls.

The waitresses had bobby socks and saddle shoes; the waiters had Elvis hairdos. The burgers had names like "the Big Bopper." And a sign said, "WE NEVER CHARGE FOR EXTRA GREASE."

GRANITE PAGE XII

Total Consistent Alignment (TCA):

Be relentlessly consistent in every word and deed.

 # GRANITE PAGE XIII

Always Be Specific

THIS Granite Page is so fundamental it should be in your mindset right from the beginning. As the Guru said in the Introduction, people are so immune to hearing companies spray the same self-impressed generalities about quality, service, selection, price, savings, and value "They roll off the human understanding like water off a duck's back." (Which the Guru stole from Brand Titan Victor O. Schwab.)

As a Brand Titan used to say, "When you stand up with specifics, you're either telling me the truth or you're a liar—and I'm hoping it's the truth." The power of specifics is the power of real examples, clear mental images, and exact description. What's more convincing:

Lower Prices or *40% Off?*
Water-Resistant Watch or *Certified Down to 200 Feet?*
Ridden by Top Racers or *Lance Armstrong's Bike?*
Scratch-Retardant Surface or *Hard as a 14-Carat Diamond?*

GRANITE PAGE XIII

Always be specific.

GRANITE PAGE XIV

The Answer Is Right in Front of Your Nose

ONE of the greatest creators of Dominant Selling Ideas was sitting in a meeting with a gaggle of clients who were theorizing about the strategic direction for a new brand. As the debate became more heated and complex, someone asked what he thought. He chuckled and said, "This is *not* brain surgery, gentlemen. If you'd look, you'd see that the answer's right in front of your nose." In this case, it was 50 percent more for 50 percent less.

Ninety-eight percent of the time, the most brilliant Dominant Selling Idea is hiding in plain sight, invisible only to those who assume that solutions must be much more arcane and difficult than they are—or are simply too close to it to step back and see the forest for the trees; the reason there will always be a legitimate need for outside marketing advice.

A classic example of this principle happened to a prominent New York City law firm that had the largest marketing communications law practice in the world. They represented three out of the four biggest international advertising agencies and had developed unique competence in a wide variety of areas that supported this industry. Their practice was twice as large as the next biggest firm in a growing global segment.

They asked us to help find their brand identity, so they could keep ahead of younger firms who were promoting themselves. They said, "Everybody knows we're *the* 'mar-com' law firm. But that's too obvious. We have eleven other practice areas as well. We want people to know that we can help in all main areas of the law with expert service."

We said, "Please understand, that's like winning the MVP in the World Series, then hailing yourself as a good athlete. There are thousands of respectable general law firms who can make that general statement. But you've just told us, you are *the #1 marketing communications law firm in the world*. Only one single law firm on the planet can claim such an honor and all the legal competencies that go with that status. You."

The managing committee was speechless, then began to congratulate one another. We thanked them. And sent them a bill for $100,000 . . .

Just wanted to see if you were still awake. We didn't charge near that. But even if we'd spent that much of their money and taken six months to research and create a dominant brand positioning, it wouldn't have been more fitting than the Dominant Selling Idea that revealed itself to this pair of Granite Page practitioners in six minutes. Look for the solution first where it so often rests, right on the bridge of your nose.

GRANITE PAGE XIV

Look first to the obvious.

GRANITE PAGE XV

Action Is Character. Brand Performance Is Your Brand

THE classic credo for movie writers is "Action is character." You are what you do, not what you say. You have to walk the walk, not talk the talk. Same for your brand.

The branding we do suggests that value awaits. We alert customers to the promise of a #1 product experience. Our communication provides a reservation for one brand parking space in the mind, reminds us to be aware upon arrival, and (in the case of image-driven brands like Budweiser beer and Chanel perfume) can even color our sense of the product experience itself. But the brand—the physical idea that's parked in the space—is the performance of the product itself and nothing less. The famous perfume must indeed smell wonderful. The designer jeans must indeed fit perfectly and feel terrific to wear. The burger must be hot and fresh. Every time. Or all the branding we do and all the Dominant Selling Ideas in the world mean zero.

A great product alone won't guarantee success—remember the Granite Page about the better mousetrap. The best products lose out to better-marketed products every day. Look no further than Microsoft. Everyone who's ever had spam, a virus, or a crashed computer has heard from his IT geek that there are far better operating systems, products, and protocols than Microsoft—everything Apple makes, for instance. So how come this is being written right now on Microsoft Word and Windows XP? Hey, we're innocent. We're victims, just like you.

But a product with a hyped promise—a bad product—is guaranteed to fail. Granite Page principles used irresponsibly will merely accelerate trial and speed up your demise.

Never take your focus off the best product you can make. Be certain that the promises you make are in alignment with performance. If your product lags behind your bold claims, adjust it in every way to match your claim. And when you can't, either change your claim or get a new product.

GRANITE PAGE XV

Walk, walk, walk. Then talk.

GRANITE PAGE XVI

Professionals Test, Because . . .

NO matter how much experience and intuition you think you have, when it comes to knowing what will work ahead of time,

"Nobody Knows Anything."

William Goldman, the great Hollywood screenwriter, wrote these three famous words about the movie business. He was describing the experts in his field—the biggest, most confident movie producers who could make a smash hit like *Titanic* one month, then go out and raise $100 million, hire a cast of thousands, and make a box-office flop the next. Mr. Goldman could have said it about any business because, no matter how sure people are that they can predict outcomes where other people are concerned, nobody ever really knows which ideas will work or won't work ahead of time. If they did, Wall Street wizards making $10 million a year to know the answers wouldn't have been telling us to buy stocks the day before the markets collapsed; the big bankers in the 1980s wouldn't have loaned billions to build buildings that no one wanted to rent, and the marketers at Coke wouldn't have tried to change its taste, nearly destroying their own brand after 150 years. The people who tell you they know what's going to happen before they try it, are lying.

Every professional knows this and is humbled by it. The original Brand Titans lived by it. We only know what works and has worked—hence all the Granite Pages. These will get us to the finals. But when it's time to predict the actual winner—to stake your life on which of your two or three final ideas will click in the heads of customers—there are too many combinations of human factors that no one can predict.

So whenever possible, we ask the target to vote. We test. Something in the results always surprises us, either positively or negatively. If we have time and resources, we can make this a big scientific affair with qualitative and quantitative analysis. Or we can call our five best customers and ask them to be candid over the phone. Anything is better than nothing, which is what most of us do. Only the mother test fails to qualify—unless your mother happens to be the creative director at Ogilvy and Mather.

So make this a resolution. An objective test, no matter how small, always improves on your golden gut.

GRANITE PAGE XVI

It's just an opinion until you test it because . . .
nobody knows anything.

GRANITE PAGE XVII

Trust Isn't Everything. It's the Only Thing

PEOPLE go to parties with people they like. They'll watch commercials and read ads from people that entertain. *But people only buy from those they trust.* That's why the age-old popular conception of what makes a great salesperson is a myth. People think good salespeople have to be back-slapping, joke-telling extroverts who are adept at making everyone their best friend. Wrong. Great salespeople actually listen more than they talk, are consistent and reliable, and think about giving their customers what they want before getting what they want. They are sincere and brilliant about creating Trust with a capital T. And as a result, customers open themselves, hand over the keys that turn on their desire, and allow the sales story to penetrate.

You have to know what we're going to say next. *It's the same for branding.* Where real brands are concerned, trust giveth and trust taketh away.

Granite Page VII, the Mouse Trap, also suggests that you have to earn trust every time. Which is why credibility, believability, reference-ability, consistency, and a primary "reason why" are such key ingredients in every successful brand.

GRANITE PAGE XVII

Create trust, keep trust, . . . and ye shall receive.

The Twelve Amateur Mistakes

On the day of his death, the Grand Guru Siddhartha Ginsu "Silver Fox" Halpern explained to me, his teenaged apprentice, "Insect, if you make no mistakes, you will most certainly fail because you are neither seeking nor striving. Mistakes are our truest teachers, so long as we heed what they tell us and hold to our quest. Now hand me a match so I can see where that gas smell is coming from."

Guru Mahatma Mahareshi "Mahesh" Goldberg

Our "wisdom warm-up" closes with a general summary of the Granite Pages, seen from the opposite side of the fence—the twelve most common mistakes successful brand people must avoid. These are the branding faux pas that neither you nor we would ever make, but of course amateurs do. This section contains advice, conveniently packaged, for you to give to others.

The Twelve Mistakes are

1. Spraying and praying . . . saying nothing by saying everything.
2. Failing to choose a Dominant Selling Idea . . . out of misplaced fear.
3. Creating a better mousetrap . . . and thinking you've created desire.
4. Entertaining, joking, singing, and dancing . . . without a selling idea.
5. Knowing all the answers . . . but never testing.
6. Breathing your own fumes . . . forgetting no one cares how great you are, they care how great you'll make them.
7. Playing inside too much when the sun's out . . . closing your eyes to the competition.
8. Forgetting that marketing is about sales . . . not marketing.

9. Being original instead of effective . . . it's not art appreciation, it's sales appreciation.
10. Chopping down your trees before they grow . . . changing your message too often.
11. Failing to simplify . . . being hard to understand, difficult to buy.
12. Forgetting your daily mantra, "It's Trust, Trust, Trust."

Parting Words

Congratulations. You now know fundamentals that every one of the world's highest paid brand professionals *should* know. But you shouldn't suddenly force every Granite Page into every brand action, any more than you should take a golf lesson and try to remember all twenty rules of the perfect swing in every shot. They'd have to pry you off the first tee.

Just focusing on any one or two puts you ahead of the game. Remember, practice makes perfect. And don't forget what the Wimbledon tennis coach said: "Bend your knees."

II. DSI University

DSI University—Orientation

A Word from the Dean

We're about to jump into the working mechanics of a core message—the Dominant Selling Idea and the simple, essential tools for expressing it. But let's pause for a moment and be reminded about where all this fits in the total brand building process.

Brand building has two large halves: Half One is finding your #1 core message in a sea of sameness. This is Rome. For real selling brands, all roads lead *to it* and *away from it*. It's the message substance that you'll pump through the communications pipeline with every dollar you spend. We start at Half One because it's as useless to have a pipeline without oil to pump through it as it is to have an Autobahn with no Beemers to drive.

Half Two of brand building is managing the executional elements needed to grow a strong, lasting brand over time. Here we're creating long-term brand equity by budgeting resources, choosing media channels, creating executions like ads and promotions, and making ongoing strategic decisions like when to line extend, when to create subbrands or split off into new brands, and how to measure success.

This book is strictly devoted to Half One, the half that gets you to the Promised Land. It has to be. Johnny's most acute problem is diving feet first into the Half Two (thinking about nifty commercials and promo ideas) without regard for any core selling idea—not realizing that without Half One, attempting Half Two is like blowing your entire vacation budget on the most expensive hotel suite in Cancun, without buying the airline tickets to get there.

Our job is to get you to the gates of the Promised Land in eight weeks or less, and that's what the process will do.

Here's how Half One works:

Step 1. Getting the DSI Right, First in Our Heads

Here we determine what our true Dominant Selling Idea should be. It's our proposed DSI, we:

1. Choose a unique ownable specialty—the specialty we can be #1 in.
2. Articulate our specialty in a brief but exacting specialty statement.
3. Propose what our ideal Dominant Selling Idea should be in the simplest, shortest possible set of words.

Step 2. Expressing the DSI so It Penetrates Other People's Heads

Here we create the core message elements that transfer the proposed DSI to the external world (consumers, media, and investors), turning it into the bona fide, living DSI. We

4. Fabricate the DSI's key building blocks to express it verbally, visually, and physically—what we call the DSI star.

5. Ring the bell to open the New York Stock Exchange on Monday. No reason not to think big.

Section II is an inside look at the big elements we'll need to bring Half One to fruition—recognizing and constructing the DSI, naming for success, and the rest so you'll be ready to fit the pieces together for a DSI that's Superlative, Important, Believable, Memorable, and Tangible—a DSI that's SIBMT. Nifty acronym, we must say.

And now . . . *welcome to DSI University!*

CHAPTER 5

Anatomy of a DSI and What to Feed a #1 Brand

Her Holiness, the Guru Mother, emerged from her meditation. "Heshie!" she said, filling me with delight whenever she chose her playful name for me, "If you want to achieve the unbearable lightness of being . . ."
"Yes," I answered, rapt with every word.
"Don't eat five slices of that coffee cake!"

Guru Mahatma Mahareshi "Mahesh" Goldberg

The Guru continues to amaze us with the parallels he sees that others cannot see. In this case it's the following: the secret of finding our real selling brand in eight weeks or less can be found in Dr. Atkins' Revolutionary Weight Loss Diet. Or the South Beach diet if you like. The key to these hugely successful programs is this:

There is good food and there is bad food (mostly processed carbs). Good food turns into lean body mass. Bad food turns into fat. So if we just eat lots of the good food and only a little of the bad food, we build lean, strong muscle, lose flab, and get the best body we could ever have—practically by default. Quality protein in high proportion is the foundation of every meal.

Sugar is poison.

Now, if you ever saw the movie *Karate Kid*, where his mentor has him paint the shed with endless repetitive strokes instead of practicing punches before the big match and the Kid doesn't know why, you may realize we're coming to an analogy here.

The point is: To achieve anything in branding (as in life), you make a choice. You choose that a hard body is more valuable to you than the fleeting taste of that coffee cake. You forget about the Nacho Gordo platter you can't have, and focus on all the good food you can have. Then you do it forever.

A #1 brand happens to you exactly the same way.

In Branding . . .
There are ideas that turn into sales and there are ideas
that turn to noise and chaff—brand building ideas
and brand wasting ideas. From now on, we'll choose
to feed our brand lots and lots of the good
and a minimum of the bad.

What to Feed a #1 Brand

Here's what you'll feed your brand at every meal:

1. Your Dominant Selling Idea. This is the good protein that builds #1 brands. You'll want to serve it in every communication. It's the creative result of Half One of the branding process.

2. Healthy side dishes to complement the protein. These are all the ingredients of Half Two—advertising, PR, promotions, and tactical activities—prepared in accordance with the Granite Pages—that support, amplify, and otherwise deliver the protein to the brain cells of our customers.

What to Avoid

As we've said, you're going to lose that addiction to sugar— brand sugar, that is—the cheap thrills and tricks sold by certain agencies as "creative," "edgy," "amusing," and "attention-getting" that, in actuality, suck power from your selling message in direct proportion to how amusing and attention-getting they are. Who can focus on or even care about a product when the subject of a commercial is a horse breaking wind which ignites like a flamethrower into a woman's face? Now, if the product was *"HorsesAzz,"* the new horse gas ignition enhancer, maybe. But this ad, as you may remember, was for beer.

Now please hear this loud and clear: We are in no way prohibiting all sweeteners and spices. As we stated earlier, clever, amusing, feel-good creative can provide heart, soul, and magic to a marketing message—but *only* when these devices move the brand story forward, sharpen understanding of the Dominant Selling Idea, and make the product an even bigger star. This is rewarding—but it takes great care and discipline to do. About 80 percent of those who try it, blow it along with their marketing budgets by acting as though grabbing attention and entertaining alone is the point of the commercial. It's only the point if you're selling theater tickets.

One of the Brand Titans once said, "If a dancing bear in a tutu does a jig on a rooftop, everyone in town will turn out to watch. But no one will be compelled to buy the house." Later we'll look at examples of creative solutions that meet the requirements for both entertaining and selling.

Official Definition of a DSI

Remember at the beginning of the Granite Pages, we described the Dominant Selling Idea as positioning incarnate? The focal point of maximum, motivating, differentiating power?

It's time to lay down an official definition to work with from here on out.

In broad terms, we explained previously that a Dominant Selling Idea is your "motivating difference"—the one difference that tips the scale in your direction versus all others at the moment of purchase.

Then we got more specific and said, "The one thing that

guarantees you a motivating difference is to be considered *#1 in a desirable specialty,* a specialty that contains all five Selling Ingredients." We call it a #1 specialty because it's:

Superlative . . . Means you're #1 at something, the best in class.
Important . . . Means that something really matters.
Believable . . . Means there's a logical reason why.
Memorable . . . Means there's an emotional hook that penetrates and is remembered until purchase time. It makes it the difference we not only need, we want.
Tangible . . . It's real; we trust it because we've experienced it and it performed as promised.

Then we added the final piece:
A specialty with all five ingredients is just another #1 specialty . . . *until it is attached to your name.* Then it's *your* #1 specialty. Then it's a Dominant Selling Idea.
And that, friends, is what it comes down to.

A Dominant Selling Idea is:

The fusion of your name and a #1 specialty in the customer's mind.

"The world's safest car" is a #1 specialty.
"Volvo is the world's safest car" is a
Dominant Selling Idea.

The DSI isn't a tag line (although if you're good, it can be, as we'll see later). It's the thought that flashes into the customer's head when she either hears your name or thinks of the specialty she needs. It's a quick and simple mental phrasing that—regardless of wording or syntax—brings together your name and your #1 specialty every time.
XYZ is (fill in the blanks):

The only one with _____. *The only one with a Tootsie Roll center.*

The best _____. *The best TV picture.*

The #1 _____. *The #1 car rental company.*

The most famous _____ for _____. *The most famous island for SCUBA.*

The _____est _____. *The fastest car.*

The _____ company. *The consumer-driven health insurance company.*

The _____ that _____. *The soup that comes with great big chunks.*

The DSI is the shortest, leanest, most succinct verbalization, visualization, or actualization (moment of performance) that rings the five bells for the Five Selling Ingredients in the target's mind.

In fact, it's worth tattooing the catchy acronym we made up for Superlative, Important, Believable, Memorable, and Tangible backwards across your forehead so that every time you sneak out to the lavatory, you'll read it in the mirror: SIBMT.

With these five ingredients, your name and specialty become a fully installed, living Dominant Selling Idea in the mind of your target. Without all five, you might generate thoughts or impressions that lead to trial—but it is not the real thing and it's not sustainable.

In the end, it all gets back to the simplest, most profound notion in all of marketing, if not capitalism: *"the difference that makes me want to buy from you."*

Our Goal

The ultimate job of all brand communication is to *propose* to the customer what we'd *like* our DSI to be in their minds. We propose it to them via our messaging using our name, tag line, visuals, and supporting claims. Then, if and only if actual performance lives up to our promise, making the promise tangible, the consumer might grace us by accepting and internalizing our proposed DSI as her own.

We shoot for the most concise possible expression to communicate our proposed DSI because that's how the brain talks to itself and stores data. Fewer words, more power.

Sometimes you can boil it down to one word. For example, *Pentium: fastest.* One descriptive word conveys four out of the five ingredients by itself. Nothing is more powerful than ownership of a single such DSI word. You're like those rare entertainment icons who are so famous, they only need a first name: Cher, Madonna, "W." Sometimes, we utilize a metaphor—a word picture or visual picture that creates an expressive shortcut and adds the crucial emotional ingredient for memorability if it's missing from the physical description alone. *Allstate: The Good Hands People.* The "Good Hands" word metaphor and visual takes the place of about fifty mechanical words to describe a reliable insurance company, adding a link that "humanizes" the idea in an otherwise dull, forgettable specialty. The "Good Hands" delivers the fourth ingredient and expresses our DSI.

And oftentimes, you can choose a name that communicates your DSI all by itself: *Diehard Batteries, The All-Star Game.*

Critical reminder: Remember that only four of the five ingredients we've been talking about—Superlative, Important, Believable, and Memorable—can come from our messaging alone. With those four, you're doing pretty well because you've successfully expressed and promised a DSI. But Tangible, the fifth ingredient, only comes from actual product performance as advertised. Only then have we created a permanent, self-sustaining DSI in the customer's mind that we can grow over time.

Why Category and Specialty Come Before Brand

A category is a grouping of products of kindred function that separates them as a class. A specialty is a singular attribute or ability within a category that's important enough on its own to sustain an entire business. A brand is your named entry in any given specialty.

We must have *categories* to have *specialties* to have *brands* for two vital reasons:

1. Categories and specialties give us context to differentiate with. This is nature's rule: Values are only defined in relation to something else. Positions only exist relative to other positions. An A student in elementary school is different from an A student at Harvard, for instance. Same specialty, different categories—different brands. Of course, same category, different specialties also enable different brands: the *chunky* soup, the *low-carb* soup. Both methods are equally effective.

2. It's how people buy. Consumers' brains differentiate and choose in a way that narrows like a funnel. To satisfy a need, our brains literally, in a nanosecond, do this:

**industry → category → specialty → #1 in specialty →
your brand name**

We can't get to the brand without first picking an industry, then a category, then a specialty, and then a #1 specialist: the brand. It's exactly like the office filing system. Our brains ask, Is the product under "F" for Food or "H" for Hubcap? If it's food, is it under "B" for Beef or "C" for Candy? People don't perceive it as a multistep process, but it has to happen before we can think of *Baby Ruth*. Filing systems are separating and organizing systems. Categories and specialties are our files.

For that reason, understanding our current category and

specialty will be a first step in determining our DSI. And engineering differences at the specialty level—creating new specialties in new categories or adjusting our current ones—will be one of our most powerful tools, as we'll see in Chapter 6.

Seeing the DSIs All Around Us—the DSI Tour

We live in a sea of marketing communication, dotted here and there with colorful floating buoys—the Dominant Selling Ideas, dropped in the water by the marketers of real selling brands. Once we start to practice spotting and identifying them, we'll notice how many there really are, we'll get familiar with their obvious and subtle characteristics, and we'll become confident that we too can float our own—so long as we maintain DSI discipline.

We're about to embark on a brief world tour of DSIs—something Australians call a "walk-about," a rite-of-passage where young Aussies leave home to observe the world all around, absorbing the wisdom of ideas and perspectives outside their own.

What's the first stop on our tour? That's a no-brainer, don't you think? Start at square 1 with the world's most famous brand names, the ones who've achieved #1, whose CEOs make the cover of *Fortune*, pundits talk about, and undergraduate courses feature. Obviously, they represent the best DSIs because they've grown so big and successful—companies like Coca-Cola, ExxonMobil, McDonald's, IBM, General Motors, Microsoft, GE, and so on.

Here's the problem:

Other than one or two of them, we probably can't say their current tag lines anymore or recall what ad campaign they're running these days, let alone where they make most of their revenue. And it doesn't matter—because they are simply *the giants*. Each with household-name status in the huge specialty it inhabits. They have mountains named after them.

61

False Start

That's why the giants are such bad *examples for us to focus on when learning to think, speak, and practice DSI.* We're not going to waste time on them because we're not going to learn anything from them. They live on another brand planet from ours. Forget 'em.

The brands we need to "go to school on" are all the companies, from #2 on down, who've created great businesses in the same markets as these giants by finding their own breakout Dominant Selling Idea, then creating a core message and product performance to match. Big companies who are not yet #1 and aspiring little companies, challengers acting like the giant brands did when they started fifty to one hundred years ago as little nothings—when each and every one found an originating Dominant Selling Idea and a new, ownable specialty that launched them on the road to become the behemoths they are now. Companies a lot like you.

Noting and critiquing the right companies is key because it's the practice habit to stay with after you finish this book— to hone your skills as an intuitive, lifelong DSI student and marketer.

So let's start with some we can learn from.

Great "Big Company" DSIs

Take any huge industry and think of the players. There is always a giant—and very often a strong #2—generally followed by a pack of names that are hardly distinguishable. But when one of the pack does emerge, clearer and larger in your mind, it means someone's attempting to get a Dominant Selling Idea into your head. And they're succeeding.

Take Rental Cars

Everybody knows Hertz (the giant) and Avis, the loyal #2— with a pretty famous positioning we might add: "We're #2, so we try harder." As memorable as it was, however, Avis's position didn't pass the DSI test because it failed the "Superlative" requirement: it didn't claim #1 status in its own specialty. It claimed to be #2 in someone else's specialty—Hertz's specialty. Avis was structurally stuck at #2 or lower, forever. After Avis, came the pack: National, Budget, Alamo, Dollar, Thrifty, Econo-Car, Payless, and so on. What differentiates these journeymen?

We can tell you that National's colored green. We get a hint from the others that they're named for economy. And Alamo? They must have been the official rental car company of Daniel Boone on his last business trip in 1836.

Then Enterprise offered the market a DSI.

It said, "We're the 'un-airport' rental company. We specialize in rentals when you need a replacement because your car's in for repairs or there's a business need. And since we know you're without wheels, TA-DAAAA! WE'LL PICK YOU UP." In their commercials, the car even drove around gift wrapped. It was a Dominant Selling Idea: The car company that picks you up.

Enterprise was clearly different from all the others in a Superlative, Important, Believable, and Memorable way. And their message stayed simple, clear, consistent, and focused.

Enterprise grew past all the other players in the airport rental counter parade, surpassing Avis as #2. According to market data, it reached higher revenues than Hertz. It's no surprise that Enterprise has now entered the airport market as well. Hertz is still perceived as the #1 car rental company. It's been the giant too long for that impression to change, and may well reclaim its #1 status again.

But Enterprise has had a spectacular run, due in no small measure to its DSI.

Take the Oil Companies

ExxonMobil, Texaco, Shell, Amoco, Sunoco, Getty, BP, Gulf, Hess. You can visualize them all lined up on Route 1 in Mahwah, New Jersey. They all sell good gasoline for the same price.

They all take credit cards and brew coffee. They're all huge corporations in the same category with no unique, ownable specialty.

You might think of ExxonMobil as the leader with the most stations. And to their credit, they work hard to maintain their brand leadership by constantly appearing first with nifty and likable service improvements. They were the first to guarantee conspicuously clean restrooms at every station—a paradigm shift if there ever was one. And they were first with Speed Pass, a mini magic wand that goes on your key chain; you just wave it at the pump to pay for your gas. Little innovations that real leaders keep on doing to reinforce the big differentiator—#1 status.

But what about the rest of them? Does anything set them apart? For all their advertising on TV, do any have a Dominant Selling Idea?

BP does. If you're under thirty, you probably don't know that for the better part of a century BP stood for British Petroleum—a global giant that was drilling and spilling, sinking tankers, fouling beaches, and promoting the petroleum culture like all the others with their stations on Route 1 in Mahwah. Instead, you now think BP stands for "Beyond Petroleum." You see their signs that look like a cross between a flower and a blazing sun. You see their ads that talk about the need to find alternative, sustainable energies. If you look deeper, you see it in every message and at every touch point up and down the organization. It's the end product of a multi-hundred-million-dollar global marketing campaign and true corporate commitment to turn one oil company into the first socially responsible, environmentally visionary and, by its actions over time, trustworthy oil company. Their DSI: The first "green" oil company. Imagine that. BP's senior management made a bold, calculated move to set itself apart with a DSI.

And by our estimation, BP's not attempting to do it on the surface or on the cheap—they're attempting to make it

Tangible by infusing it through every aspect of the organization. They built out their new core message by adjusting their name, creating a simple, supporting tagline, recasting their entire visual identity, and creating a compelling story around the brand. Last but not least—they committed to Total Consistent Alignment (TCA), endeavoring to "become" the brand internally and externally with every action, communication, and initiative over time. They're walking the walk that leads to tangibility.

Creating brand-changing DSIs for behemoth corporations with millions of customers who've locked-in impressions of the specialty and brand over decades is a far more complex, long-term play than it is for smaller companies. BP wasn't planning for mass overnight acceptance of an oxymoron—a "green" oil company. It will happen with relentless consistency and focus over time—something BP is showing all the signs of executing. Great brands, with all the benefits that accrue, become #1 by using the principles to create legitimate DSIs that deliver all five of the ingredients. There's no reason to expect BP to be the exception.

One More: Auto Insurance

We have some good news. We just switched to Geico.

Geico picked a no-nonsense, Dominant Selling Idea: "the 15 percent cheaper auto insurance by phone."

Then they drilled it into everyone's head. They tempered their relentless messaging with just enough humor and variety to avoid the tedium of so basic and unglamorous a message—but they never failed to center these messages on their pure DSI, either. So on the day our insurance carrier ticked us off enough to switch, we picked up the phone. Their DSI achieved trial. Then, when they answered the line in two rings with a real human, and were so efficient and courteous in the sign-up process, they closed a sale.

It didn't hurt that we smiled over the years at Geico's commercials. But we never would have picked up the phone without that DSI switching itself on in our brain at the precise second of need—unlike the hundreds of other insurance companies whose names didn't register, even though we'd heard just as many of their commercials. And we're obviously not alone because Geico, a relatively obscure name a decade ago, has become the #1 direct writer of private passenger auto insurance in the United States.

Take the DSI Tour down Main Street

Let's take a walk through the most dynamic DSI laboratory in the world—small business, USA.

Some of the most creative, effective DSI examples anywhere are originated by the dedicated, energetic entrepreneurs who run businesses, teaming with direct competition that they drive by every single morning on the way to work. They're operating more often on instinct than professional brand training, thinking about differentiation every single day because there's no coasting. Survival depends on it. The DSIs they come up with often would be the envy of any Fortune 500 marketing department and most would do well to study them.

Pizza a Slice Apart

As we start down the street, we notice four different pizza shops: Tony's Pizzeria, Nick's Pizza House, Pino's Pizza Village, and this one: *Pepe's Brick Oven Pizza—Real Brick Oven Taste in Every Slice.*

Pepe has a Dominant Selling Idea: The brick oven pizza place. We walk inside. There are those ovens blazing away, the rustic Italian décor, and pizzas that look a little lopsided—definitely handmade.

As a matter of fact, restaurateurs as a group are some of the world's most natural DSI marketers because they have to be.

There's too much competition and too little brand loyalty—you're only as good as your last meal. So from inception, restaurants pick great names and distinctive central themes—then use atmosphere, décor, menu, wait staff, pricing, dramatic locations, and more to differentiate every aspect of the business. Think of your five favorite restaurants and you can recount what's unique, important, and memorable about every one.

A Twist from the Massage Therapist

On the second floor of every building that has a pizza shop is a therapeutic massage business—one of the fastest growing personal service businesses in America. There are superb massage services offered by Bob, Patty, Sharon, Richie, Suzanne, and Michelle. How in the world do you differentiate a massage practice other than word of mouth?

Ask Michelle. Her sign instantly flags us with one of the truest DSIs we've ever seen. Michelle has some Native American ancestors. Her practice is called Native Palm and her tag line is "My heritage is in my hands." When you enter her office, you're surrounded by a Native American ambience from the art to the background music. She has developed lotions containing ancient ingredients she's studied. Needless to say, there's a warm, natural, earthiness laced with Native American spirituality exuded here—along with a terrific massage.

No other massage business in town looks, feels, or sounds like Native Palm. No one else could claim the same DSI: massage with Native American spirit. Michelle told us that in massage school, they'd assured her it would take two years to build enough clients for a full schedule. Six months after opening her doors, Michelle has a fourteen-day wait for new customers.

Ideas in Storage

If our feet aren't too tired, let's check out the seven self-storage facilities over on Self-Storage Row. A dull, undifferentiable specialty, right? Totally—except for this one called Fortress. It's got a three-story, cube-shaped building with concrete walls, no windows, and parapets like a castle's on the top. Its tag line is painted in big letters on the side: MUSEUM QUALITY STORAGE. And if that isn't enough, they've wrapped a giant inflatable padlock and chain around the whole building! The place and its Dominant Selling Idea are simply unforgettable: the safest storage company. You couldn't think of a more secure place if you tried.

Differentiate This Date

And finally, while we're sitting in our car contemplating getting a massage from Michelle or wood-fired pizza from Pepe, we hear ads on the radio for four different Internet dating services—all sounding alike, all promising romance. Except one. It stakes an ownership claim on the mother of all romantic end benefits that the others don't: marriage. eHarmony. com, with its free test that measures "twenty-nine key areas of compatibility," promises me nothing less than a soul mate for life. Its ads feature one blushing testimonial after another, all from brides—Becky, who married Robert; Jenny, who married Steve; and Zoe, who married Zack (having a first name that begins with "Z" was their twenty-third key area of compatibility) to prove their Dominant Selling Idea—*eHarmony is the one that gets me married.*

Learning to Spot Brand Sugar— the Ultimate DSI Messaging Test

The flip side of "DSI spotting" practice is looking at all the weak, ineffective messages drifting around on this sea and to make value judgments about what's wrong and why. This isn't being cynical or derogatory, it's gaining a fuller understanding by studying both sides of the coin.

All you do is stand a brand up to the DSI messaging test. The test has three questions. To pass, you need a 100 percent score:

Question 1 (the Golden Question): Is the key message expressed Superlative, Important, and Believable?

Question 2 (the Substitution Question): Can I take out the company's name, plug in anybody else's, and have the exact same ad or claim? Or is it a claim that only this company can make?

Question 3 (the Star Question): In communications like advertising, is the product the star of the ad or incidental? In other words, if the communication is Memorable, is it for the right reasons? As an old Brand Titan once sarcastically pointed out, "When you've got nothing to say, sing it!" A good rule of thumb is: the sillier, the more intricate and involved the entertainment shtick and the more incidental the product, the more the advertiser is compensating for lack of DSI. We just saw a True Value Hardware commercial the other night. A numb-looking guy comes out the front door to find his lawn statues gone and his car missing. The rest of the commercial shows the lawn statues driving his car down a desert road—presumably escaping to Mexico. In the last five seconds, we find out: (1) The lawn statues were embarrassed by the guy's unkempt yard. (2) They left home because of it. (3) This is a True Value Hardware commercial. (4) At True Value, you can buy things like rakes and fertilizer for improving your lawn.

Thank you, True Value. That was funny, but when it comes time to repair my lawn, I'll head down to my local hardware place where they also sell materials for improving my lawn because, they, like you, are a hardware store.

Practicing with the DSI Test

True Value failed Questions 1, 2, and 3 (the Golden Question, the Substitution Question, and the Star Question). OK, it partially passed Question 1 because it's Believable that a hardware store sells lawn stuff.

Let's look at some other examples:

Circuit City—We're with You. Fails at Questions 1, 2, and 3 in our opinion because, frankly, isn't everybody? Our plumber would say he's with us when times are rough.

Boston Market. Originally it was named Boston Chicken before it was bought by a larger corporation to be taken national. Indeed, they have the juiciest, best-tasting chicken in the world. You want to eat the world's best-tasting chicken. And if the cook's that good, you'd expect to like the stuffing, ham, meatloaf, and all the trimmings she made, too. Then they changed their name to Boston Market. Not only are you seldom hungry to eat a market, you'd hardly be moved by this tag line: *Boston Market, Slow Down.* Isn't that a road sign? Failure in all questions.

Would we have reached for the phone to call *Northwestern Mutual Life, the Quiet Company* the way we grabbed the receiver to call Geico? Maybe if we were shopping for earplugs. But where's the offer, the promise, or even one of the eight Human Appeals?

This is great practice. Put the brands you see all around you to the ultimate DSI messaging test. It'll help you capture all five ingredients when it comes time for yours.

CHAPTER 6

The DSI Templates: Eight Ways to Be #1

Class come to order! "#1" is not a casual term. It's a professional term of art with a method, a structure, and a strategy. As Vince Lombardi's cousin in advertising once said, "#1 isn't everything, it's the only thing." It's what we live or die by. You, sleeping in the back row, would be advised to become an expert.

Guru Mahatma Mahareshi "Mahesh" Goldberg

We've described a Dominant Selling Idea as your name attached to a specialty you're considered #1 in—the thing you do that's superlative, important, and believable, made memorable and tangible, which is also the "motivating difference" that makes people want to buy you. We've just taken a quick tour of a few dozen bone fide DSIs. The difference they manifest is simple and obvious to the eye and ear. They wouldn't be DSIs if not. But soon it'll be our turn to come up with our own DSI. So we'll start with a basic question:

How, in Practical Terms, Do You Gain #1 Status in a Specialty?

How is a "motivating difference" put together and preempted to be your very own, especially when others are competing in the same business? Is there a structural mechanism or set of rules for mentally moving one brand ahead of another in the mind; for co-opting the #1 specialty that's the heart of a DSI?

Yes, and it's the place we begin.

Constructing hundreds of DSIs over the years, we've found that there's a catalyst or mechanism that helps set your DSI up for #1 status by default. It's based on one of two practical strategies. With each strategy, you get four different DSI templates to choose from, making a total of eight that follow.

To set you up for these templates, you need a brief understanding of the steps by which categories and specialties sprout . . .

The Specialty Tree

Specialties grow on trees.

The category is the trunk. Specialties grow out of the trunk like branches. Then keep branching off those branches. For example, if the original category is rubber tires, here's a little fable to illustrate:

Once upon a time, there was just one tire manufacturer. So for a brief time, the category and the specialty were one and the same. That probably lasted until 1881. When the first branch sprouted, it might have been . . . truck tires. Again, when you're literally the only one in a specialty, you're #1, the best, the one and only, and most popular by default. To this day, being the only one in your specialty is still the only automatic, no-brainer way to be #1. But sooner or later, if your business has any merit whatsoever, you will get competitors.

And so it was that not too long afterward, next to the original truck tire branch, three additional competitors sprouted. They all seemed exactly the same. Until someone who envisioned this book, decided to set himself apart from the others by *specializing within his specialty* to reach a perception of #1. He didn't have to invent a whole new specialty to do it, either. Listening to his customers, he discovered that there were four key, preexisting attributes that people already expected within the truck tire specialty (like four little buds on the specialty branch): "high mileage," "low cost," "ruggedness," and "safety."

Indeed, in any specialty, this is the short list of benefits, traits, or performance specs that customers want most.

He saw that his competitors, like him, were pretending to be all things to all truckers. None of them were claiming any of those key specialty attributes as their own. So, intuiting the Rules of One from the Granite Pages, he chose just one to declare as his chief attribute and #1 specialty—the one his customers wanted most: high mileage. That meant his new #1 specialty would be "high mileage truck tires." He named his products accordingly, focused his messaging, and then made sure that he produced rubber compounds and quality construction that delivered the undisputed highest mileage for his customers. He suddenly pulled in all the customers who wanted high-mileage truck tires.

Soon the three other competitors caught on. One chose to own key attribute 2 (low cost) and acted accordingly. One chose safety. And so on.

Now there were four happy #1 specialists in the truck tire business, each with a maximum share of the market that corresponded to their customers' needs.

And then one day a new truck tire maker germinated next to the specialists' branches. He looked around for a key, pre-existing attribute to claim as his #1 specialty to make him famous. But in the truck tire specialty now, all the seats in first class—high mileage, low cost, ruggedness and safety were taken. There were no more sweet little buds on the branch.

If he wanted to be #1 in a specialty, he had to invent a new key attribute for truck tires or sprout a whole *new kind of specialty* off the rubber tire tree trunk to be best in.

It just so happened that his rubber compounds were bullet proof and he had friends at the army base. He realized he could make truck tires specifically designed for the needs of a different market with a different kind of truck: *Military truck tires*. A new specialty branch was born. Suddenly he had no competitors and lots of customers. He was #1.

The Moral of the Story

Nature's crystallization of specialties follows pretty regular steps. The eight DSI templates that follow are proven, practical gambits you can use to formulate or preempt an ownable, #1 specialty, heeding these basic steps:

Step 1: Be the only one. The #1 failsafe way to be #1 in a specialty is still the old tried and true: be the only one who does it. This is the status that inventors or the truly first to market enjoy. But often this step isn't available to you because you have competitors or you've come to market later. In that case, you skip Step 1 and proceed to Step 2.

Step 2: Grab an "attribute bud" for your very own. Since every specialty has that preexisting, generally accepted set of key attributes that are considered more or less inherent to the product by stakeholders, this is where you start when you're not a candidate for Step 1. Earlier we called them "buds" on the specialty branch. For example, in cars, the preexisting attribute buds are things like: speed, gas mileage, handling, safety, utility, luxury level, reliability, and country of origin and so on. What you do is grab any one of these attributes that's not already taken—starting with the most important one available. By claiming it with vigor, that bud sprouts into your own branch and your own #1 specialty, your specialty within the specialty.

Theoretically, there's no limit to the number of attribute buds you can find or develop. But practically speaking, there are only so many that really excite buyers. When they're all taken, the specialty's full. You can join it, but not be #1 in any important aspect of it. At this point, you proceed to Step 3.

Step 3: Sprout a new specialty. (See Step 1.) When all the attributes are taken, invent a new specialty to be the first, only, and #1 in—essentially, going back to Step 1. This isn't claiming an attribute bud on the same branch. This is moving to a whole new branch off the trunk. Again, whether you're actually carving out a whole new specialty or just preempting a really big attribute in the old one is a matter of judgment. But here's a good test to determine one versus the other:

Staying in your current specialty carves out a more defined slice of your current market. Your customers come from the same pool as before and share the same basic needs, and your main competitors don't change.

On the other hand, creating to a new specialty expands you into different markets. Customers share an expanded or different set of needs and you're open to a new set of competitors as well.

Think of it this way: Any customer with a truck wants tires that are high mileage, low cost, rugged, and safe to some degree. A military customer with a truck is in a different market because he has a different group of needs. Low cost and even high mileage may be meaningless to him. He needs bulletproof, desert-heat resistance and special sizes for a completely different set of vehicles. You've moved beyond the general truck tire attributes to a new specialty.

Final Caveat for Specialty Attributes: Finding the Sweet Spots

Nothing is more important in the quest for your #1 specialty than choosing which key attributes provide the most traction to differentiate with, and which are either too minor or—this is important—*too major* (i.e., too broad-ranging and overarching to have practical significance for customers to be able to measure and identify with). In other words, there's a Sweet Spot where an attribute or performance spec is neither too big to grasp nor too small for customers to care about. Just right.

Here's a case in point:

Rookie salespeople are always taught it's not features but benefits that customers care about. Trainees are told how to recognize the basic difference between features and benefits; then instructed not to dawdle on features, but to focus on how each one improves the life of the customer (that is, on its benefit). Good advice.

The theory is that you can start at any feature and string together a progressive series of benefits until you reach the ultimate benefit.

All right, that's fine in theory—*just don't go too high into the stratosphere* or you'll lose your customer in the ozone. For example, ever hear the old saw, "People don't buy a drill bit, they buy the holes it makes"? OK, but by that logic, if you play out the ultimate string theory, it also means that people are really buying the better fitting pieces of furniture that the precision holes will ultimately create. And that must mean they're buying the nicer feeling on their derrieres when they sit on the furniture made with the tighter tolerances of the better holes that the drill made, and . . .

Put on the brakes. In real life at the drill rack in aisle 3, no experienced salesperson would be swimming that far downstream. Instead, they'd be talking at the tool level—about sharpness, heat resistance, durability, size, and price because that's the level of feature and benefit the customer can relate to. For drill bits, those attributes are in the Sweet Spot. The customer knows that if he gets those attributes right, all the rest will fall into place when it's time for holes. An exciting feature like "nanoceramic coating" that yields 30 percent extra sharpness and 50 percent more heat resistance—that's a benefit that's measurable and meaningful, and that's the level where I'm making my purchase decision on $5 drill bits, not derriere comfort.

Obviously, the drill manufacturer should choose a brand specialty in the Sweet Spot as well. Try "the World's Sharpest Bits."

Ultimately, the Sweet Spot for key specialty attributes differs from product to product and is a matter of your judgment, experience, and what prospects specifically tell you is important to them when they buy. If you were selling vacation property, indeed you should stand there and paint verbal pictures of hypothetical sunsets and family gatherings in the future because your product is much more than the dirt and weeds under your feet. Your product is the dream, and that dictates your Sweet Spot.

Sweet Spots for Big Companies

Finally, as you'd expect, it's far more challenging to choose a Sweet Spot when you're a big, multifaceted, corporate brand with profound influence up and down your customer segment, than if you're seeking the Sweet Spot for drill bits. A global drug company may know that consumers generally value the attributes of "access to medicines" and "caring," but may judge that these are too lofty, too far out of the Sweet Spot to own or to gain traction in the consumers' mind. They might judge the Sweet Spot to be at a more specific, tangible level like "calling me up and talking": "The Company That Calls and Talks to Me," for example. Remember "The Car Company That Picks Me Up"? By selecting and communicating that level of attribute, consumers would then associate the company with broader notions like "caring." But it wouldn't happen if the company had tried to tell consumers, flatly, "We care." It's as imperative if not more imperative for big, complex companies to find and develop their Sweet Spots. It just may take some extra thinking, care, questioning, and commitment.

Eight Practical Ways to Own a #1 Specialty— the DSI Templates

We'll now take the basic steps and strategies and turn them into practical tools that we can nail down #1 status with. The main rule is: always follow the path of least resistance. Assess honestly and realistically where you are now, then take the straightest, most obvious path to an available #1 spot. It may be tempting to declare a whole new specialty as a big, dramatic way to set yourself apart. But you don't always have this option or this need. If you're in a specialty where none of your competitors have positioned themselves, which is amazingly common, don't switch your specialty. Pick off the choicest attribute bud and offer the world your Dominant Selling Idea.

Now, take a look at the most common templates successful brands use to capture a #1 specialty for later service as a Dominant Selling Idea. One of them will become yours.

DSI Templates 1–4: Staying in Specialty

1. The Preemptive Attribute DSI

Because it is template number one, we'll state it one more time for the record: Preempting one generally accepted, key attribute by announcing exclusive ownership before others do, is probably the most direct, time-honored way to snatch yourself a DSI within your specialty.

If you have the attribute, you can claim the throne just by sitting in it first. If you're a ski mountain, you can be tallest, steepest, or snowiest.

The danger in being King of Attributovia, however, is that you can be dethroned easily if your attribute is based on too quantifiable a metric—low price, for example. You get knocked off the minute someone beats your number. So choose one that's more flexible and defendable—more qualitative. In cars, luxury, design, and handling are more in the eye of the beholder and easier to maintain than speed, price, or crash rating.

2. The Magic Ingredient DSI

Also known as the fairy dust, this gambit is based on a special ingredient apparently not found anywhere else in the specialty— a perception that's usually reinforced with a magic-sounding coined name. It's really an invented label for a key attribute that sounds like something everyone should have. It was a traditional favorite in the golden age of packaged goods on TV and was made into an art form by many of the Brand Titans. Halls throat lozenges had "Vapor Action"—menthol in other words. Halls didn't try to change specialties—it was still an over-the-counter throat lozenge sitting on the rack next to nine other brands. But it became the only lozenge that gave you *Vapor Action*—a product based DSI that eventually made it the number one selling brand as well. Nike made "Air" into its own magic ingredient and a Dominant Selling Idea for years. Although not a coined name, "Air" is a coined concept. Of course, the quality and importance of the fairy dust is determined by your target market. A software manufacturer set itself apart because it claimed to be the only one with *Stage III Architecture.* It may not mean much to you or me, but that was a Dominant Selling Idea for the IT people who were buying online financial services software for banks at the time.

3. The Sleeping Beauty DSI

This variation of the magic ingredient above is a classic gambit in which you feature a superlative attribute, ability, or ingredient that all the others in the specialty also possess but never considered important enough to even mention. It's hidden in the deep woods but it's there nonetheless, waiting for its prince to come. As the first one to release it, of course, you preempt it and set yourself apart. One of the classics was a campaign that Shell gasoline ran for years. Shell's DSI was "the extra-mileage gasoline" because Shell had Platformate. The commercials showed a car without Platformate running out of gas. Then a car with Platformate drives hundreds of feet farther. What Shell didn't tell you was that all gasolines had Platformate. It didn't matter. Viewers remembered that Shell was the one with Platformate, and Platformate made your car go farther.

4. The Golden Metaphor DSI

Sometimes your specialty is simply perceived as so dull or such a commodity or necessary evil by the average customer, no superlative attribute you can find will elevate you to memory, unique interest, or credibility in the target's mind. In other words, you can't create a Dominant Selling Idea because you can't get past the Superlative, Believable, or Memorable parts of the DSI test. In this case, you need to attach yourself to an emotion-evoking metaphor based on one of the eight human appeals. A metaphor is the Pentium chip of poetry—the expression device that says one thing is like something else, something I already know and presumably love—connecting even the most boring of products into the emotion circuit with all the good things that go with it. A strong metaphor is impossible for your competitors to copy and can be impossible to forget for your customers. It can be verbal or visual.

Fortress, the self-storage place in our DSI walk-about, used a Golden Metaphor ("Museum Quality Storage") to become distinct and memorable and then reinforced it with a visual metaphor (a giant inflated padlock attached to the building). Canned vegetables are notoriously dull, soggy, and boring. But the Jolly Green Giant attached the visage and persona of a big, green, happy character who became a visual metaphor for goodness, wholesomeness, trust in quality, likability, and even freshness in canned vegetables. Coors Beer still promises "a taste of the Rocky Mountain high country."

The Golden Metaphor is the one gambit that doesn't always become evident at the core messaging stage of brand development—Half One of the long-term branding process we defined in the introduction to this section. It often gets revealed in Half Two—during the expression and executional phase when talented copywriters and art directors are laboring to bring extra life to the DSI. When a great, inspired, DSI-inducing metaphor is discovered downstream of the core messaging process, be flexible enough to fold it back in retroactively—bringing naming, logos, tag lines, and all the core elements into alignment with the Golden Metaphor.

DSI Templates 5–8: Creating a New Specialty

When someone else is in command of the #1 status in your specialty or its key specialty attributes, we use the "Captain Kirk" Rule from the Granite Pages—we invent our own new specialty and, in so doing, become #1 in it. Again, there's no mathematical science to this. But generally, a whole new specialty changes the game in some way that preempting a mere attribute can't, by adding or realigning attributes to suggest a new class of performance or utility for a whole group of products. In 1899, people tried to classify the car as a "horseless carriage," a carriage with a specialty attribute. But automobiles were too big an idea for that. They were changing the game. So when it's really a whole new specialty, it's usually important enough to push you into new markets, not just a greater segment of your current one. Some people say a laptop is just a specialty of PC desktop computer. But this is being written on a laptop at thirty-five thousand feet in seat 12A, an hour before landing at JFK, and we say it's a specialty in its own right.

5. The "2 Mints in 1" DSI

Just like the name suggests, in the "2 Mints in 1," we create a new specialty by merging two present ones together, giving birth to a new offspring. We named this template in honor of a historical classic, the legendary Certs Mints TV commercial. In it, two actresses argue until the announcer settles the issue by naming a new specialty, making them both happy.

ACTRESS ONE
"Certs is a *candy* mint!"

ACTRESS TWO
"Certs is a *breath* mint!"

ANNOUNCER
"It's 2 (CLICK), 2 (CLICK), 2 mints in 1!"

With that, Certs claimed a new specialty and the DSI that went with it—the candy mint that cleans your breath.

Another great classic created by the Brand Titans was Palmolive Dishwashing Liquid. Until then, washing dishes was every woman's invitation to "dishpan hands." Then Palmolive said, "Our liquid has such a gentle formula, your hands actually get softer and more feminine the more you use it! It's like hand lotion and dish detergent in one." Their great DSI was encapsulated in their tag line: "Softens hands while you do dishes."

Subaru was an average station wagon that happened to have four-wheel drive like an SUV. It realized that a large number of its buyers wanted SUV utility without SUV gas guzzling or massive size. So it put the two categories together and became the SUV Wagon.

Movies are sold in Hollywood using the "2 Mints in 1" all the time. Hollywood execs think in categories. They want to make original films and copy past success at the same time. So when you sell a film, you tell them, "The high concept is, it's *Big Chill* meets *Animal House*," or "It's *Rambo* meets *Father of the Bride*." Two successful concepts merged into a new one.

6. The Transplant DSI

Here you create a new specialty by borrowing an already understood, accepted, popular specialty and transplanting it into your own. It's not a merger of two equals to create a new third the way you did in the 2 in 1. You're putting your current specialty on steroids by imbuing it with an entirely new power and instant credibility—changing its nature but still keeping a portion of its original name and identity as the anchor.

Until a year ago, 911 emergency call handlers were using pencils and paper and thumbing through loose-leaf manuals to advise panicked callers in crisis. A company called Powerphone was the first to create computer software that would automate the old system of call handling. The problem was, Powerphone had no credibility in computer software. Buyers assumed they had just put the old paper manual on a screen—when in fact the software was intelligent and interactive. It could save lives.

What Powerphone's market already did understand and love was a specialty called CAD—Computer Aided Dispatch software. CAD had successfully computerized the dispatching part of the 911 process over the past decade and was in general use all across the country.

So Powerphone borrowed CAD and did a transplant into its own specialty. It heralded its software as the arrival of CACH (Computer Aided Call Handling). That is, call handling with a major CAD transplant; call handling at computer speed. The market "got" the new specialty and the Dominant Selling Idea and CACH took off.

Bill Gates made a famous speech in 1995 when he proclaimed, "Banks are dinosaurs." The implication was that Microsoft and its friends were going to render banks obsolete by the following Monday. The bankers were startled awake and went crazy. They began falling all over themselves to create PC banking online to avoid what they euphemistically called being "disintermediated." Ironically, the first place they turned to for software was the dark side—Microsoft and Quicken, the only ones who had personal financial software working and available that the banks could co-brand in a hurry. Other big organizations like VISA began offering products as well. The banks were giddy with the idea that they could service customers from home for pennies a transaction versus dollars for live tellers—and still charge the same fees. Maybe this computer thing wouldn't be so bad after all.

But right away, there was a problem. Average customers weren't adopting it at the double-digit rates that the analysts were predicting. They weren't buying it at all. Only the geeks and financial compulsive types were because the software looked, sounded, and was . . . complicated. You had to read a hundred-page manual. You had to be someone who liked balancing a checkbook. Eighty-five percent of all customers never balance their checkbooks. How do you reach that 85 percent?

A tiny new company called Home Financial Network decided to invent a new specialty—Easy to Use Home Banking Software. For credibility, of which they had none, and for instant DSI impact (that is, to pass the Superlative, Important, and Memorable test), they went looking for a transplant. How about the only personal electronic banking legacy that had ever succeeded and by now was a trusted, beloved universal product: the ATM machine? Everybody had an ATM card in their wallet. Everybody knew how to use it. Nobody had to learn anything. The ATM told you what to do right on the screen.

So the little company with a staff of nine employees did an ATM transplant into PC banking software. They called their new product Home ATM. They said if you can use an ATM machine, you already know how to use Home ATM. They told the banks, "Now you can have an ATM in every home," and they made the product look exactly like an ATM machine on the screen, right down to the big buttons.

Everyone started talking about and remembering the "one that's like an ATM." Banks wanted to be customers. In three years, the little company had 150 employees and was sold to a Fortune 500 company.

7. The Spin DSI

Whenever you hear news reporters talk about "the spin" Democrats put on a Republican story or "the spin" Republicans are putting back on the Democrats, all they're attempting to do is old-fashioned positioning. Spinning is saying, "Think of it the opposite way. In another context, it's entirely different." In fact, the perception becomes brand new. "The president was seen shoplifting a donut from the Krispy Kreme across from the White House when witnesses saw him place it in his pocket and leave without paying." Or "The president was making an eloquent public statement about the national obesity crisis by personally removing one symbolic donut from circulation and rendering it full of lint, thereby suggesting there are more appropriate food choices for children."

Che Guevara was either a terrorist or a freedom fighter, depending on whether you went to Princeton or NYU.

DSI-level differences are manufactured this way all the time. In one obscure, squalid region of India, they grow a grainy crop called flea seed. Because of the unique temperature, humidity, and soil quality, this is about the only place on earth flea seed can grow. Most people we know wouldn't be thrilled to be in the same room as a flea seed, let alone put it into their bodies. But flea seed has an amazing property—it is probably the best natural source of digestible, soluble fiber in the world.

Astute brand marketers didn't add or alter a single attribute of flea seed. All they did was rename it and spin: "Pure Psyllium: The doctor-recommended, all-natural fiber supplement, medically proven to lower cholesterol and prevent cancer while keeping you regular each day." Sounds like it was discovered by the guy who invented penicillin, doesn't it? You don't find something like this in Bangladesh next to the water buffaloes. You find it at Walgreens, next to the laxatives, with a brand name like Metamucil.

Imagine selling "diet beer" to steelworkers in Ohio. How far would you get? About as far as the other early failed diet beer brands like Gablingers. Then Miller made a diet beer and spun.

Miller said, "This isn't beer for diet sissies. This is the one beer for guys who love beer so much, they want to drink even more. It's regular beer—same great taste—it just doesn't fill you up." So where previously you could down ten beers at a sitting, now you can down twelve to fourteen. What's not manly about that? They reinforced the message with testimonials from guy opinion leaders—ex-athletes like Dick Butkus. Just like that—spun, done, and number one.

Another of our favorites is pork, a meat with a bad rap if there ever was one. The poster child for saturated fat, high cholesterol, sulfites—you name it. Pork's elected representative in the mind is bacon, followed by honey-glazed baked hams. Wouldn't be health food.

Now take your mind off bacon for a minute and consider this: Pork loin, roast pork, pork chops, and the like are nutritionally quite lean—comparable to poultry, in fact. You know you love the taste—now you can give yourself permission to eat it by thinking of it this way: *"the other white meat."* As you can see, this is a spin with a bit of a specialty transplant as well. There's no rule against combining or overlapping DSI templates, as long as it works.

And then there's the prune. It made you think of wrinkles, crabby old ladies, and the heartbreak of constipation. Then the California Prune Board asked us to think about prunes another way. They said, "A prune is really a plum!" Who knew? A delicious, dried plum! Well now . . . that's a horse of a different color. Kind of purple to be exact. Just like that, prunes were repositioned forever in our heads with an entirely new DSI. In already well established categories, spinning is a particularly good way to revitalize products by exorcising old negative brand equity and simultaneously creating a new DSI.

8. The Pure Original DSI

Finally there's the great classic—creating a new specialty by inventing something entirely new and great that no one's ever seen before. This kind of a DSI is much more product and invention driven than marketer driven, although the impetus to invent it can come from a strategic needs analysis of the marketplace (research into what people need but don't have now). When the product and its specialty are genuinely new out of the box or even revolutionary, the performance description speaks DSI all by itself. You simply need to name it and say very clearly and simply what it does, to set yourself apart.

The technology industries are inherent incubators of pure originals. They're new-invention industries by nature. Think of the Sony Walkman, the Palm Pilot, the Blackberry, the iPod, eBay, and Salesforce.com.

But technology also innovates and generates competition so fast, specialties can get away from the inventors before they can establish a #1 brand like iPod, for example. DVDs changed the home theater specialty. HDTV changed TV—but no one was able to establish a proprietary hold. The technology was uncontainable.

Packaged goods and food manufacturers create pure original specialties all the time through constant R&D effort. The Swiffer is an entirely new kind of cleaning implement with its own action verb. You don't sweep it, you "Swiffer" it. It's not a vacuum or a broom or a mop. It's an original. It's a new product and a new specialty, and its DSI is automatic: the only Swiffer. Power Bars created an energy bar specialty. Pop-Tarts were a new breakfast specialty.

Because of the difficulties of new product development and their high degree of failure, creating pure originals is probably the most unpredictable way to get to a DSI. Again, it's more product development driven than marketing driven. But once you've got a winning original, the DSI process is quicker and more straightforward than the others. Your specialty and your DSI are already decided by your revolutionary new performance spec. Find yourself a great name and take it from there.

The Templates Are Not Mutually Exclusive

As we conclude our discussion on the templates, we should point out that none of them are islands unto themselves. In practice, they're frequently combined and overlapped to powerful effect. For example, along with being a "2 Mints in 1," Palmolive liquid was also a classic "Sleeping Beauty DSI" because other dishwashing liquids also contained hand-softening ingredients to prevent chapped red hands. Palmolive was simply the first to call it out, claim it and ride it to #1. Shell with

Platformate was a "Sleeping Beauty" DSI but it was also a "Magic Ingredient." Use the individual templates as a guide, not an inflexible mandate.

Corporate Conglomerate DSIs Versus Single-Industry and -Product DSIs

We won't kid you. Some specialties are easier to come up with than others. Identifying a single representative specialty for big corporations with scores of products and lines of business is hard. By definition, they have multiple major differentiating facets that must be coalesced into a single, overarching idea of value that somehow passes the test of Superlative, Important, Believable, Memorable, and Tangible. Not many succeed at it. That's why big corporate tag lines are generally diffuse, platitudinous softballs. They're often lofty and aspirational. The CEO may be convinced that declaring "A Passion for Excellence" will set his conglomerate apart as the only one with passion and excellence, but the guy in the skyscraper across the street would argue it. And the prospect would say, "I'm glad you espouse a value like democracy or control or innovation, but I can't respond to ideals. I need names, numbers, and facts to be Superlative, Important, and Believable." Remember Granite Page XIII: *Always be specific.*

So when you see the rare, successful big corporate DSI, it's generally built by focusing on a specific proprietary aspect or an original superlative attribute that is carried forward as a symbol of a larger identity. We call it "leverageable specificity." Here's an example:

Prudential Insurance Company's timeless "Get a piece of the rock" was a brilliant metaphorical expression highlighting one superlative attribute among many the company had to offer. Prudential was the first large "mutual" insurance company, meaning that its policyholders shared in the equity of the corporation, earning dividends. The DSI was "The big insurance company that gives me shares."

But even though Prudential is a huge corporation, it is still known as a single-industry company: insurance. If you're a multi–product-line conglomerate brand like GE (which makes light bulbs, dishwashers, and locomotives) or Mitsubishi Heavy Industries (which makes ships, planes, cars, and electronics), you're going to be stretching the envelope of DSIdom. GE owned a famous tag line, "We bring good things to life." People remembered it after GE advertised it for years. It added a notion of warmth to the image of a giant equipment maker. But apply the three-question DSI test and tell me if it was just a nice slogan or a motive difference that stimulated an impulse to do business? You're right, it's the former. Now GE has a new CEO and a new tag line: "Imagination at work." Our reaction is "We're happy for you. So what?" Is there something I'm supposed to buy here? Can GE or any conglomerate create a real DSI for its corporate brand?

You can, as long as you understand that you're going in with limited options and you can resist the urge to waste time and money, forcing your corporate brand to do more than it can do.

ATT has recently made a laudable attempt at leveragable specificity with its current tag: "The world's networking company." We give them credit for assuming a #1-in-specialty position. Unfortunately for ATT, after all their fits and starts and failures in the past two decades, this claim may ultimately not get past DSI Test Question 1—it simply may not be believable to anyone outside ATT.

For other smart multiheaded giants, the path to corporate identity lies not in spinning their wheels trying to differentiate the conglomerate, but in the development of signature product brands that become so powerful and attractive that the giant corporate parent derives its identity by association with them as the maker of [blank], or the people who bring you [blank] versus the other way around.

Procter & Gamble, the world's greatest packaged goods marketer, is famous for not investing in brand building for the

P&G flagship. All you need to know is that P&G is the maker of #1 brands like Tide and Crest—and P&G absorbs all the brand status it needs. Kellogg's has been a famous and beloved brand for generations, not for itself, but because it's the company that makes my favorite cereals: Sugar Frosted Flakes, Fruit Loops, and Rice Krispies. That is Kellogg's DSI.

Closing with the Classics

Let's wrap up our DSI walk-about with a look at the great classics—the ones actually invented by the Brand Titans themselves and their associates at the dawn of the television age. By the late 1950s the Brand Titan Rosser Reeves had invented the concept of the USP or unique selling proposition. Our concept of the Dominant Selling Idea is simply an updated version of the USP, designed to accommodate more varied sales channels and media than were available in Rosser's time. But the big principle—that every brand must find one core idea, own it exclusively, and center the brand on it relentlessly—was originated by Rosser and will be the cornerstone of brand power until brands are obsolete.

Armed with USP principles, amid the exploding arena of packaged goods advertising on television, and blessed with a genius for word play that was common in an age when words mattered to our culture more than electronic images, the Brand Titans created a golden age of DSIs expressed in great DSI tag lines. Each of the following brands were the first to make the specific propositions offered below. For example, Rolaids, not doctors, invented the term *acid indigestion*. They then reinforced these messages relentlessly for decades, preventing any competitor from displacing them at the summit, burning the DSI into the mind for generations.

> M&M's . . . The Milk Chocolate Melts in Your Mouth, Not in Your Hand.

Halls Throat Lozenges . . . With Vapor Action
Visine . . . Gets the Red Out
Greyhound Bus Lines . . . Leave the Driving to Us
Allstate . . . You're in Good Hands with Allstate
Wonder Bread . . . Builds Strong Bodies Twelve
  Ways
United . . . Fly the Friendly Skies
Rolaids . . . Stops Acid Indigestion
Hebrew National Franks . . . We Answer to a Higher
  Authority
Wheaties . . . Breakfast of Champions
Clairol . . . Only Her Hairdresser Knows for Sure
Maxwell House Coffee . . . Good to the Last Drop
Crest . . . Recommended by Dentists to Fight Cavities
Morton Salt . . . When It Rains, It Pours

The DSI brand marketers who created each of these had the advantage of individual, well-named products with superlative attributes that were available for ownership. They also enjoyed national advertising budgets in a less cluttered era. But none of that takes away the fact that they focused like a laser on one clear differentiating idea of value that they could own and expressed it consistently over time. And notice one more thing: Nearly every one of these tag lines employs an artful Golden Metaphor that infuses the idea with emotion, memorability, and fun in a way that is the *opposite* of faux branding: they never fail to make the product the star. To a lover of DSIs, these are objects of rare beauty—not to mention profit and #1 market share. What made them great then matters as much if not more today.

Choosing Your DSI—Is This the One?

By now you should be feeling more intuitive about what DSIs look like and sound like—better able to tell pure protein from brand sugar and processed carbs. So you should also be getting a little nervous. How are you going to come up with yours— separating the real big one from the three or five possibles that you're sure to get down to.

First of all, you can rest assured that the steps for getting there—from the actual questions you'll use in your fast-track market research to plotting available specialties, and so on— are what the eight-week DSI process is all about.

As an example, here's the kind of scoring test you can use later on when you're down to your finalists and you want the winner. It's really a checklist based on the Granite Pages and common sense. It's a guide, not a mandate. Your gut still gets two votes.

Ten Decision Criteria for Ranking DSIs

Criteria	Rating 1–5 (Best)
1. Superlative: Can you perform this function as well or better than anyone else? Is it something you can do best?	1 2 3 4 5
2. Simple, understandable, and relatable: Is it quickly obvious as a superior proposition with key benefit associations? Is it too high level, or is it in the Sweet Spot?	1 2 3 4 5
3. Preawareness level: Does it point to a solution the target already knows it needs? If education is required, is the point simply grasped?	1 2 3 4 5
4. Importance: Does it address a top issue for decision makers?	1 2 3 4 5

5. Believable: 1 2 3 4 5
Is it credible for us to say? Do we have a
logical "reason why"? Will the market perceive
that it's within our domain? Does it connect
with our prior competency?

6. Measurable: 1 2 3 4 5
Does it lend itself to objective measurement
not only by customers but by us so we can
gauge progress and improvements?

7. Ownable: 1 2 3 4 5
Is it a proprietary, or is it available to be
exclusively ours?

8. Protectable: 1 2 3 4 5
Are there barriers to entry or can we erect
them?

9. Feasible and affordable: 1 2 3 4 5
Is it feasible to make real and tangible by our
actions in a realistic time frame? Do we have
the technology and expertise, or can we afford
the investment to get it and deliver what we
promise?

10. Marchable to: 1 2 3 4 5
When all is said and done, will our people
march to it, rally around it, embrace it, and
accept it as a legitimate compass to guide the
business at large?

Three Little Words . . .

As we conclude our DSI guided tour and you take a moment
to rest your feet, we want to implore you not to forget these
three little words:

Practice makes perfect.

As long as you're in business—which means you're in marketing, which means you're in sales—never stop observing and admiring and deconstructing the DSIs all around you. Put every ad you see on TV or in magazines or billboards to the DSI test. Compare the booth headlines at trade shows. Make subjective value judgments. Why is that message great? How exactly is it Superlative, Important, Believable, Memorable, or Tangible? What is that one missing? WWGD?! (What would Guru do?!)

And look again at all the examples in the past two chapters and try to pinpoint the actual delta that triggers the difference— The Safest Tire, Museum Quality Storage, The SUV Wagon. Which of the eight templates did they use? What do they all have in common? We think you'll agree that every one is simple, specific, direct, obvious, and presumptive of #1 status.

This is how you hone your instinct, reflexes, and craft in DSIs.

Now we'll turn to the five building blocks of the core message—the five core parts of expression for real selling brands that we'll fuse together into a full-dimensional, self-reinforcing DSI.

CHAPTER 7

DSI Expression:
The Five-Point Star

And as the three wise brandingmen turned the corner at Madison and 44th, a star suddenly shone in the heavens, more luminous than any before. "Was it a prophesy?" wondered the first. "Was it that fourth martini we just enjoyed at Wollensky's?" pondered the second. "No," declared the third, "It's the light in Mr. Reeves's office. He's just come up with another great selling idea!"

Guru Mahatma Mahareshi "Mahesh" Goldberg

The transference from proposed DSI in our heads to a real DSI in other people's heads is the job of the *Five-point DSI star,* the five core messaging elements that physically express and install your DSI in your target's mind. The five-point star is different from the five selling ingredients contained in a #1 specialty. The ingredients are a series of qualifications and tests that lead you to your proposed DSI. The five-point DSI star is built *after* you find your #1 specialty and DSI. It's comprised of the primary elements of expression that the outside world will see, hear, touch, and feel to grasp your DSI and bring it to life. The five points of the star are, in this order,

1. Your name
2. Unique ownable specialty
3. DSI tag line
4 Key visual
5. DSI-level performance

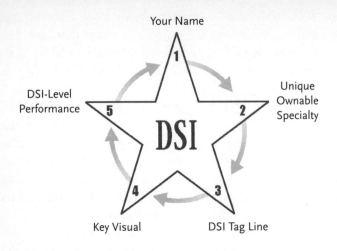

You can think of the DSI as the center of this star with your name at the top, followed by the Unique Ownable Specialty and so on. The prospect's mind starts at your name and travels around the star, clockwise. The actual moment of DSI recognition—that "AH-HA" moment when his brain registers, "Superlative, Important, and Believable," and connects them to your name for the first time—can occur at any of the five points on the star. That's when the DSI star lights up—like the ball that drops in Times Square on New Year's Eve. Our job is to build all five points in succession. Even if the star is able to light up at point 1 or 2, we always complete all five points so we can achieve the brightest, most impactful star possible.

Moment 1 or 5, It Just Has to Jive

It doesn't affect the quality of the DSI if the star lights up at point 1 or it takes all five points to get the light to go on, as long as it happens.

For example, your DSI can first register when someone hears your name alone (point 1) when it's uniquely descriptive and evocative. "Invisible Fence," the electronic barrier for dogs is one example. Another is "EZ Pass," the automatic toll-paying device available for vehicles in New York and New

Jersey. "Ball Park Franks" is another. As we'll see when we get to naming, it's marvelous to construct a name that launches your DSI instantly each time it's said or heard—and we'll always attempt to do so—but not all products afford you this special opportunity.

Other times, the DSI first registers at point 2. For example, the Empire State Building is a strong, evocative name. But the DSI doesn't occur until you travel to the second point of the star—the Unique Ownable Specialty. That is, New York's tallest skyscraper. The name 747 was easy to say but meaningless by itself when it was introduced in 1969. Until they attached its exciting new specialty: Jumbo Jet. Lights on at point 2.

One of the greatest Dominant Selling Ideas of all time occurred at point 3 of the star—the point we call the DSI tag line—that is, a tag line that expresses a selling idea, not just a cute slogan. The name M&M's is meaningless by itself. Add point 2 (the idea of little, hard-shell, multicolored chocolate spheroids) and you get closer. But it took star point 3, the DSI tag line "The Milk Chocolate Melts in Your Mouth, Not in Your Hand," to evoke an unforgettable Dominant Selling Idea that's made the candy a top seller since World War II, when it was invented as a convenient way to get chocolate candy to the troops.

One of the most famous cases of a DSI happening at star point 4, key visual, was Master Lock, which used to fire a rifle bullet through the lock to show it would hold, no matter what. That unforgettable image fused the name, its description as the toughest lock, and the tag line together into a full DSI package. Another famous example of a DSI occurring at the key visual point was the early Band-Aid ads. An image of the Band-Aid sticking happily to an egg in boiling water said it all. And then there was Timex. They would put the watch through a torture test—drop it out of a plane, run over it with a truck—then cut to a close-up and "tick-tick-tick-tick-tick." Being a brand classic, the announcer would close with a great DSI tag line: "Takes a Licking and Keeps on Ticking." But you already had your DSI, "the most dependable cheap watch," when you saw it fall out of that plane.

Finally, there are the times when the DSI occurs at the moment of trial and use—point 5 of the star. A personal favorite is one of America's fastest growing ice cream shop chains, a company called Cold Stone Creamery.

Our kids raved about it before we ever got there or heard about it. They said, "They mix the flavors for you right there, right before your eyes! It's so much fun." We thought the name was intriguing but not meaningful—until we went to the shop the first time.

There, behind the counter, was something never seen before in an ice cream shop. A refrigerated granite stone counter, several feet wide, upon which the servers plop down a slab of ice cream for every individual customer, then mix in any of one hundred different ingredients displayed right in front of you, making your own customized flavor, fresh on the spot.

Now the name Cold Stone became descriptively brilliant and unique for us. But since we'd never seen a marketing message or an advertisement and their name suggested nothing inherent about ice cream, it was the product experience that created the Dominant Selling Idea in this case: "The one ice cream shop that mixes your flavor on a big, cold stone." You walk into this DSI.

Like any rule, the five points aren't without exceptions or overlap. The DSI moment can come in between points. Your name might get you 80 percent there, but you need your description or the DSI tag to create the emotional twist that lights the star.

Again, in nearly all cases, you'll want to use all five points in a seamless expression package, no matter where the moment actually occurs. All five points create reinforcement, follow-through, and resonance for your DSI that add to its power and durability. Even if you've got a name as great as "Invisible Fence," you need a unique ownable specialty, a DSI tag, a key visual, and product performance to deliver your strongest, most fully actualized Dominant Selling Idea to the prospect's heavily bombarded mind.

Over time, all great DSIs will eventually register at point 1, becoming intrinsic to your name through long, consistent association. IBM used to be a meaningless set of initials. Years ago, International Business Machines probably achieved its DSI at point 5. But after years of hegemony as a #1 brand with a three-letter nickname, IBM triggers a DSI as the world's #1 computer products and services company by initials alone. Someday, your #1 brand will do the same. But for now, we're focusing on creating your Dominant Selling Idea in the first place. And it will occur at some point in your construction of the five-point star.

Building the Five-Point Star

There's a natural order to building your DSI star, just like building a house. Foundation comes before walls, walls before roof, etc.

Here's the order we'll follow:

(1) We'll confirm what we think is our current specialty. (2) We'll list the key specialty attributes and the degree that we possess them. (3) We'll define our competitors' specialties and prospective new specialties. (You'll learn how to do this in Part Two.) (4) We'll choose our #1 specialty based on the above by applying a simple scoring test. (5) We'll write a two- to three-sentence Specialty Statement that articulates our unique, ownable specialty and our primary "reason why." (6) We'll reduce it down to our proposed DSI. *Only then do we create a name for our brand.* Naming always follows the choice of your Dominant Selling Idea because your name will ideally launch your DSI or at least support your DSI whenever it's spoken.

We know what you're saying. "I already have a name." In that case, you make a strategic decision whether it will be more profitable for you to keep it or to rename yourself to match your Dominant Selling Idea. They are your two most critical branding components and they must reinforce each other.

After you've chosen your DSI and name, we'll continue until we've created the remaining points of the star:

We'll pick a catchy, memorable name to identify our Unique Ownable Specialty if the specialty doesn't already have one.
We'll create a DSI tag line.
We'll create a key visual when appropriate.
And finally we'll concentrate on point 5, DSI-level performance: what you do and how you do it that makes your DSI a tangible experience. We'll achieve it by focusing on Total Consistent Alignment (TCA)—adjusting specific product features and performance to align with the proposed DSI wherever possible so it's reflected throughout every aspect of our business.

Know Where the Star Lights Up

A key to creating the five-point star is to get the DSI moment to register at the earliest possible point, even though every point counts and the whole star will eventually be completed. For example, we'll always shoot for a name that sets off our DSI at point 1. Depending on our circumstances, if our best possible name is not enough to light up the star at point 1, we'll create a name for our Unique Ownable Specialty out of catchy, descriptive words and attempt to trigger the DSI by point 2. If we're still not there, we try to light the star at the DSI tag in point 3, and so on. It's critical to know at what point the DSI actually lights the star for two reasons:

1. This forces us to push every point to the max—making each as succinct, specific, and powerful as it can possibly be.

2. Once the DSI star is lit, we use the remaining points of the star to reinforce—making the DSI as resonant and powerful as it can be.

It's important that you build the star in our numerical order. It's not that you can't build a house starting with the roof, it's just so-o-o inefficient. We're often in situations in our consulting practice where excited clients, thinking about the prospect of a new, powerful brand, come to the first working session with detailed, scripted ideas for the killer TV commercials they want to make. If you recall from the Twelve Amateur Mistakes, this is #4. Get your DSI right, first. Then head downstream.

Now lets set the record straight on naming.

CHAPTER 8

DSI Star Point 1:
Fun and Names

I would have liked to see John Wayne named Dick Trickle. Or Frankenstein named Frank Steinway. Do names matter? I THINK soooooo.

Guru Mahatma Mahareshi "Mahesh" Goldberg

Ouch. The Guru sounds a little revved up on this one. But with good reason. Naming has a pretty exalted seat in the royal throne room of the real selling brand. In fact, if you think of your Dominant Selling Idea sitting on the throne, your name sits right in its lap. Like Mini Me. It's so important, every other part of the core message stands to the side. And yet, oh mystery of life, it is so often wasted as a brand asset by so many companies—it's the chief cause of the Guru's acid reflux disease and causes him to reach for his Extra Strength Mylanta.

As you'll remember from Granite Page II, there is no sweeter sound to a person than his own name and no more important sound to your brand either. Try advertising, let alone thinking about a brand without a name. You can't. It's literally the first thought we have in the mental sequencing that constitutes a brand idea; the handle we remember. That's why a great, descriptive, memorable name is the most fortuitous moment to launch your DSI—in the first nanosecond—right at point 1 of the DSI star.

Great namers shoot for that goal every single time.

And then there are the not so great namers.

The Stupid Hall of Fame

There is a statue out in front of the Stupid Hall of Fame that greets all visitors to the shrine, located behind Miracle Cleaners in Athol, Massachusetts. The statue commemorates a seminal branding event that was too profound to be marked by a simple plaque in the hall: *the Stupidest Corporate Naming Decision of All Time.*

This name is a work of art. Actually conceived—although we've never been able to verify it—with the help of one of New York's top branding identity firms, who were paid handsomely in American dollars. We want to say to the parties involved, who may feel aggrieved when reading this, we think you can sue us but you won't win because we're expressing a personal, subjective opinion about a property in the public domain. If you do win, you'll have to take down your statue at the hall, disappointing tens. So let's be mature and think about the readers.

The company is an executive jet charter firm that provided an absolutely first-rate service and had very satisfied customers. It was originally called eBizJets—not a bad name, considering it was about jets, business customers, and a business model that let customers book charters quicker and cheaper online because the company could search thousands of affiliated charter operators to find you a plane at the right place and time. eBizJets had a unique, new specialty—"aggregated charter"—and was competing effectively with the "fractional ownership" jet companies like NetJets who were much more expensive. The business grew into a leading player.

Then came the name problem. Someone claimed prior ownership of the eBizJets trademark, challenged, and won.

The company began a name search. They looked at thousands of logical possibilities that would flag them instantly in prospects' minds as the nation's premier, aggregated jet charter travel company. And after careful consideration, they chose their name: "Sentient."

Not Sentient Airlines. Not even Sentient Jet-a-Rent. Just . . . Sentient.

Why on earth would you volunteer to do that to yourself? Why would a company with an elite, sexy product, building awareness in a viciously competitive market, seek the honor of meaning absolutely nothing by name—permanently forfeiting the entire first point of the DSI star? In fact, it was worse than zero. A name like that starts your brand in a huge hole. You're not even in a category! While your competitors are instantly ID'd and already off selling, you're still at square 1, having to explain why you're not a burglar alarm company, a consulting division of Deloitte, or a bank merger. Now imagine a senior executive team, a board of directors, and, we fear, a reputable brand identity firm all voting yes to this, and you can see how they got a statue in Athol, Massachusetts.

The only possible reason we can think of for such a move was because the CEO or someone else thought it sounded like an auspicious, important, big-company name since so many other companies at the time were going public with concoctions like Agilent, Altria, Quatanex, Trivergis, and Flatulent. The only quarter those companies get is that they are either multidisciplined service providers, technology companies with products that can't be described in English anyway, or former outlaws who don't want anyone to know that they used to be a cigarette company. A "jets" company has no excuse.

After Sentient, honorable mention goes to all those who deliberately choose initials instead of words to name or rename companies. This disease has been rampant in the past ten years. They'd have statues too, there are just too many of them.

CVX, GDW, TYC, AGT, CYA, ORD, RKD—the last two are also airport codes. They all might as well be. The same diatribe used for Sentient can be used here. These are a license for your company to mean zero, forcing every other part of your core message to start by climbing out of a hole, then have to work a whole lot harder.

IBM and GE

Yes, we know. But remember, they didn't start that way. It took them generations before they shortened themselves— mainly because their customers had been nicknaming them for years. And they had literally billions of dollars to reinforce name recognition with. You don't.

Great Names

Instead, give your brand the gift of a great name. In order of priority, great names are

1. A direct statement of or highly supportive of your DSI
2. Descriptive, evocative, or colorful in some way
3. Ownable by you
4. Easy or pleasing to say

You already know some of our favorites in the brand world: DieHard Batteries, Invisible Fence, EZ Pass, Ball Park Franks. Here are a few others: Egg Beaters, Rainex, Ringling Brothers Barnum and Bailey Circus, Stealth Bomber, Oreck 8 Pound Hotel Vac, Honey Baked Ham, Butterball Turkey, Godzilla, Frankenstein, SuperBowl, TGI Fridays, RollerBlade, Chain Link Fence, ZIP code, No Fat–Low Fat Restaurant, Sam Adams Beer, Head & Shoulders Shampoo, Home ATM Software, Hefty Trash Bags, Ziploc Sandwich Bags, Instant Breakfast.

Nearly every one has a complete DSI built right into the name, launching its brand rocket on sound. Say the name and say the selling idea. You can't even separate one from the other. How incredibly efficient.

Ringling Brothers Circus may sound like an exception, but it's not. It's on the long side, but it is so colorful, ticklish to the fancy, downright fun on the tongue—it is an ownable, unforgettable circus of words that say, "big, exciting, entertaining circus." Had a pretty good tag line to go with it, we might add: "The greatest show on Earth." Brand Titan stuff.

Names like this are not always possible for lots of practical reasons we've mentioned earlier. It's fairly easy to name a new fruit candy that squirts when you bite into it: Gushers. It's harder when you're dealing with complex, industrial, or high tech products, for example. And sometimes, all the descriptive words in your specialty have simply been taken. But you always keep the goal and you always strive to connect your name and your DSI.

Coined or Made-up Names

Even made-up or tech names can be inspired when you keep the great name criteria in mind. *Compaq* computers, the first portable PCs, was a perfect example. You couldn't miss the sound of their unique, superlative attribute, could you? Compact. The drug companies make up amazing names that alliterate or hint their way to descriptive meaning. Viagra and Levitra are two. Viagra has *virile* and *aggressive* in it. Levitra has *levitate*. (They're both drugs for erectile dysfunction, of course.) We always hear that the naming companies who specialize in these names use computer programs that spit out thousands of these things. They plug in a couple of root words and the variations pop out. We've never actually seen one of these programs, but there's no reason why you can't do it yourself. If you're naming a new male performance enhancer, think of a list of descriptors like "virile" and "aggressive" and "levitate," or maybe "Debby" and "Dallas." Stay away from words like *wilt*. Then mix, match, and switch syllables until you come up with the next Viagra.

When You Start with a Given

When we already have an established corporate or family name as a given—like Oreck or Halls or Johnson & Johnson—we can often borrow and attach a seamless descriptor that becomes fused onto us, said in the same breath, essentially becoming part of our name. Look at the amazing amount of useful selling information in the name–descriptor combo Oreck 8 Pound Hotel Vac. Halls lozenges attached Mentholyptus, making their product Halls Mentholyptus. The shampoo from Johnson & Johnson that doesn't cause tears is fused together as Johnson's Baby Shampoo.

When we don't have the possibility of a descriptive name, we choose as memorable, musical, or metaphorical a sound as we can—and set our sights on lighting the DSI star at point 2 with the addition of our Unique Ownable Specialty. Remember 747: the Jumbo Jet.

The Naming Tour

Of course, great names are by no means limited to brands. Going on a naming tour to practice seeing and hearing the great as well as the ungreat names is excellent cross training for the up-and-coming namer. What makes each name great or ungreat? Nine times out of ten, it has to do with the four criteria for great names above.

Take Movies and TV Shows

The movies are a fun place to start. Smart Hollywood execs always ask for the name before you get a chance to pitch because they know the power *Animal House* or *The Godfather* have to instantly evoke anticipation in the hearer and be remembered by the word-of-mouth promoter. If you'll notice, the following all fit at least one of the criteria for great names: *Rambo, Heaven Can Wait, Rocky, Fatal Attraction, Casablanca, Diehard, Tarzan of the Apes, Twilight Zone, The Wizard of Oz, Honey I Shrunk the Kids, The Day the Earth Stood Still, Psycho, Ben Hur, The Gladiator, Titanic, Moonstruck, Bachelor Party, 12 o'Clock High, Scarface, Debby Does Dallas, The Parent Trap, The Omen, Field of Dreams, Star Wars,* and on and on.

They are specific, descriptive, emotive, tantalizing, frightening, metaphorical, unique sounding, idea launchers. Tongue ticklers, never tongue teasers.

Now, of course, *The Good, the Bad and the Ugly* is both a good title and a reference to the fact that there are thousands of really bad movie names that are just as worthy of your consideration—names that are empty, flat, and invisible. A video store tour will show you about one thousand of these in ten minutes: *It's My Turn, He Said She Said, She's All That, The Boost, Talk to Me, Moment by Moment, Time and Again.*

We're tired already. Invisible does its job, making them harder to remember. Not all the bad titles are bad movies or flops, and vice versa. Good just gives you a lot more horsepower. Occasionally a good movie can even get killed by a bad title. *The Shawshank Redemption* was a hard-to-pronounce, meaning challenged, weird set of words for a really great movie. It was mediocre at the box office—though it later flourished once it hit video stores because word of mouth had a chance to build over time. But its name held it back needlessly during its theatrical run.

Finally, the namers of TV shows are the true masters at quick, cut-through naming because they have to be. There's no $15 million ad budget and not much time to advertise a show—especially a one-time shot like a miniseries or a made-for-TV movie. So there's no messing around with subtlety or poetic inspiration. The title has to tell the audience everything it needs to know in five seconds: i.e., "This is a violent domestic drama, with sex, crime, and a twist to make it different from the two hundred others you just watched—on next after

Temptation Island, followed by *Desperate Housewives."* On TV you get *"The Texas Cheerleader Murders," "When Good Pets Go Bad,"* and *"Beverly Hill's Grandma: Profile of a Hooker."* As Alan King once said on NBC's *Tonight* show, "If Shakespeare pitched *Hamlet* to the networks, they would've changed the title to *Murray and the Ghost."* We're sure they would have. These guys know what they're doing. They may be crass—but they're great namers.

Strategic Naming: When and When Not to Name

Take the time and effort to get the greatest possible name for your company, your flagship product, your proprietary process. Then stop. Remind yourself of Granite Page III, the Universal Paradox *("In every aspect of the branding process, less is more."),* before you go on to name other aspects of your business, supporting products, or services. In other words, just because names are so important, don't get name happy and start over-naming. We recently had a client with thirty-six different trademarked names for service features attached to the main product. Like any laundry list, the sheer numbers defeated the purpose of great naming, which is to focus the mind on a single, descriptive, proprietary handle. Instead, this torrent of names was a jumble of self-created clutter. We eventually packaged thirty-six names into about six to a collective sigh of relief both inside and outside the company.

Rule of thumb: name only what is truly proprietary and pivotal to your overall brand. That usually means your company, key product or service depending on where you want your brand focus, and one or two specialty attributes, properties, or ingredients.

Audi, the first all-wheel–drive luxury car maker, named its unique traction system Quattro because it was the heart of its engineering and driving difference. Mirage parachute containers come with Alien Technology, the unique harness system that conforms to your body, giving you more flying control than any other rig. Intel was smart enough do the name thinking for its customer partners ahead of time for the benefit of both parties. It named its penultimate computer chip Pentium, created the Intel Inside seal, then furnished it to manufacturers so that they could highlight this gold-medal ingredient as a symbol of #1 quality.

In real branding, nothing is sweeter, more powerful, or more efficient than a great name. Just be careful not to suffocate your DSI by surrounding it with too many of them.

Last but Not Least,
Beware the "Richard Dick" Trap

Don't pick a name if you don't like the nickname it comes with! After a while, everybody will try to expend .0073 calories less when saying your name by abbreviating it with initials or a nickname. This isn't a bad thing, once your brand is firmly established after decades of dominance. Minnesota Mining and Manufacturing was OK going to 3M. But it would've been bad if their initials had spelled out some unfortunate term, as was the case with the venerable First Unitarian Church of Kennebunkport, ME.

Don't name yourself Richard if you prefer not to be called Dick. And don't name your insurance division, Premier Insurance Group, either.

CHAPTER 9

DSI Star Point 2:
Articulating Your Unique
Ownable Specialty

*The fundamental question for some of you is "Are you a man or a
mouse?" And if indeed, you are a man, then the question becomes
"Are you a girlie-man?"*

Guru Mahatma Mahareshi "Mahesh" Goldberg

Moving on to point 2 of the DSI star, our task will be to
choose, articulate, and then give a distinctive name to our
Unique Ownable Specialty—the specialty we're #1 in.

By now we know we must always decide on our specialty
before any other element of the brand, even our own name,
because our brand name must be reflective of our specialty
whenever possible. And since the customer's mind can't even
get to our brand name without passing through our specialty
first—we have to think of "shoes, casual, outrageously priced"
before we can think of Bally or Mephistos—giving our specialty its own catchy, cogent name boosts the chances a customer will find her way to us. When she seeks out a related
specialty, she'll more likely remember our memorable specialty name—our "handle" if you will. And once directed to
our specialty, she'll land on our brand.

Small boat motors were an undifferentiated category until
Ole Evinrude popularized a specialty named the Outboard.
Once boaters learned the new specialty existed, they sought

the specialty by name, whether or not they'd heard of the brand name. "I want an Outboard motor," was all they had to think or say. That impulse led to one place in 1910—an Evinrude brand outboard. Specialty and brand combined to make each other famous.

Choosing and Articulating Specialties

It's a good confidence builder to keep reminding ourselves that the number of specialties in the world is limited only by the imagination and the eye of the beholder. Aircraft is a specialty in the category of mechanical transportation. Jet is a specialty of aircraft. Fighter is a specialty of jet. Stealth is a specialty of fighter. These branches can go out as far as they have any material differentiating significance to any segment of the market.

And finally, remember that technical agreement on what's a category, a specialty, or just a superior attribute doesn't matter to anyone but brand intellectuals. If you want to declare that your new superior difference creates a whole new specialty, or not, you have a perfect right to do so. Regardless of what you or anyone else calls it, it's going to be your specialty.

Advancing and Receding Specialties

Creating a legitimate new specialty when you need one (because the top attributes in your current specialty are all occupied) is easier than you'd think because specialties are designed to sprout up from existing ones—like an extension ladder that's raised, rung by rung, or, as we waxed previously, a tree that sprouts branches. This is a daily part of evolution. As new specialties keep appearing, older specialties recede in importance, still useful as general descriptors but no longer relevant for differentiating a selling message.

The automobile began as its own distinct specialty in the transportation category, relative to horses, buggies, and bicycles. In your town, all you had to advertise was "automobile," and your specialty was powerfully defined. But the industry quickly grew and "automobile" needed layer upon layer of new specialties to accommodate all the new products and competitors: "luxury car" like Cadillac versus "aspiring professional car" like Buick versus "Everyman's car" like Chevy. And so on. "Luxury car" soon divided into "American luxury car" and "European luxury car"—then "British European luxury car" and "German European luxury car"—then "British European sport luxury car" (Jaguar) and "British European elegant luxury car" (Bentley). If that looks like a complex family tree, look at the specialty evolution of SUVs in the past five years.

Today, "automobile" separates you from "horse" or "boat"—but has receded too far down the tree trunk or down the ladder to differentiate you any more for selling purposes. And it's all due to the inexorable advance of specialties.

Structure for Articulating Your Specialties

You'll notice that the above examples have a simple structure in common: they're all composed of a base specialty plus a key descriptor word or words for the attributes that "extend" them until they reach their ultimate defining point—their #1 specialty. In other words,

Base + Extenders = #1 Specialty.

"Athlete" is a base. "High jump" or "high jumper" is the extender. "Olympic" is the next extender. "Gold Medal" might be the ultimate extender, making your #1 specialty "Gold Medal Olympic high jumper." If "car" is the base, "sports" or "luxury" would be the extenders that separate us into the next level of specialty. With complex specialties, just keep adding extenders until you separate yourself from all others in the base specialty—just far enough to be standing alone in the Sweet Spot that's materially apart from the others, the #1 spot.

Eventually, when you get far enough away from the base specialty, the base shifts to a new, higher plane, as well. Building on a favorite example, "airplane" was the original flying machine specialty. The first jet was called a "jet airplane": extender + base. But as jet technology overtook the aviation world, "jet" advanced beyond "airplane" to become a new base. "Fighter planes" became "fighter jets." "Passenger planes" went to "passenger jets." "Jumbo" was a new specialty extender when the 747 first appeared and, with no competitors for decades, "jumbo jet" remained a unique, ownable specialty for the 747: base + one extender. Then Airbus entered the picture with its own, even bigger jumbos, "super-jumbo jets": base + two extenders. A new specialty was born.

In short, the more competitors in and around your specialty, the more extenders you'll need to articulate your #1 specialty.

Who Determines the Base?

It's the same as above: conventional wisdom. "Jet" was so dramatic a shift, it overtook the airplane in the collective mind. It took a few years but "car" eventually supplanted "carriages—horseless and horse drawn," becoming generally accepted as the vehicular transportation base. The base can also advance quickly on a technology paradigm shift. Phonograph records died almost overnight. The new base became CDs. ("Britney just put out a great new CD.") At some point, a new mode of transportation will replace the car and we won't call it a car. We'll ride in the family Hovercraft. We'll have luxury hovercraft and sport utility hovercraft. Same extenders, new base.

Naming Your Specialty

Station Wagon, Mini-Van, RV, SUV, Sparkling Water, Sparkling Wine, Fire Hose, Panty Hose, Pope Mobile, Sno-Mobile, Roach Clip, Roach Trap, Diet Cola, Un-Cola, Flip-Flop, Fanny Pack, Tudor Mansion, McMansion, Sports Bar, Hybrid Car, Jumbo

Jet, Jumbo-Tron, Luxury Box, Bobbi Socks, Bungee Jump, Heat Pump, Wine Spritzer, Elliot Spitzer . . .

As with every point of the DSI star, we'll strive for the most succinct, memorable set of words to name our Unique Ownable Specialty. We're aiming to light the DSI star at point 2 with this specialty moniker, if it hasn't already been lit by our product name at point 1. Attaching a brief, descriptive, appealing name for your specialty is one of the most reliable triggers for any DSI in the minds of the marketplace—on a par with your product name itself. For example, if you'd built the first supermarket in a town full of grocery stores, all you'd have to do is call yourself Bob's Supermarket to establish your DSI with all the shoppers in town who already know they want the specialty "supermarket" when they go food shopping. The Unique Ownable Specialty is what lights the DSI star in this case, no disrespect to Bob.

Practice

Like everything else, we can practice our specialty naming skill. Take any product or company you can think of and articulate its specialty, starting with the base and adding all the extenders until you nail it. Now think of its specialty name like outboard motor, laptop, or minivan. If it doesn't have one, create your own, using unique, colorful, and memorable words like "Jumbo" jet or "Monster" truck whenever you can. Again, there are no absolute right answers, and practice makes perfect. Debate your assessments with branding colleagues. You'll be more confident and better prepared to pinpoint your competitors' specialties and stake out your own when we get to creating your own DSI.

CHAPTER 10

DSI Star Point 3:
Tag Lines

Tag lines these days are like the stuff you find at tag sales. They're throwing it away, but they have the chutzpah to try to sell it to you before taking it to the dump.

Guru Mahatma Mahareshi "Mahesh" Goldberg

Tag line is the trifling term for what used to be, not so long ago in branding history, one of the most powerful, shimmering aspects of DSI messaging. Today, its art and application seem all but lost. The term has indeed become what its name implies—a pleasant-sounding slogan *tagged* onto a brand or pasted below a logo—a feel-good aspiration or superfluous throwaway. It need not be.

In the hands of the Titans, a tag line was designed to be a precision-cut selling gem, the catalyst for your entire Dominant Selling Idea, infusing your name or logo with instant selling power on sight. A tag line was your DSI gift wrapped in a magic word package, signed, sealed, and delivered to your mental doorstep. A complete DSI instant breakfast for use on billboards, the side of your building, next to your logo, on golf shirts, business cards, or the employee kitchen wall, making any place it appeared a selling place. Such a word collection we call a *DSI tag*, and that's what we're now after.

You can take the "great names criteria" from Chapter 9 and

with a couple of tweaks convert it to the "great DSI tag criteria" to tell if a line is a fluff ball, a slogan, or a real DSI tag.

The next time you see a tag line, and especially when you are creating one for yourself, ask

1. Does it directly state or specifically support the DSI? (Read: does it promise a difference I want to buy?)
2. Is it ownable? (I.e., could another company substitute its product name for yours and say the exact same thing?)
3. If the answer is yes to 1 and 2, then is it evocative, colorful, or phonetically memorable?

OK, class. The following tag lines were ripped from today's advertising pages. Are they worthy of greatness or the card table in the driveway at your next tag sale?

With You All the Way. Driven to Excellence. Ideas for Living. Leading the Way. Expect Something Extra. We Mean Business. A Passion to Achieve. Inspired to Do Great Things. Putting You First. Doing What We Do Best.

We see you're all vigorously raising your hands, even in the back row because you've been practicing DSI spotting so diligently, igniting debates among your colleagues, spouses, loved ones, and clergy.

"Every one of them fails the ownership question!" says an attractive girl in the front row. "No DSI," I see hastily written in marking pen on a sign. "There's no specific offer or promise!" someone else says. "They're talking about themselves, not about what they'll do for me!" gasps a hyperventilating student before fainting in the aisle.

Our response is "Correct, correct, correct, and correct." What we need to do is getting rather obvious by now, isn't it? Into the weak broth listed above, throw in

"Join the Navy and See the World."
"Please Don't Squeeze the Charmin"
"Prudential: Get a Piece of the Rock."

"Federal Express: When It Absolutely, Positively, Has to Be There Overnight."
"Ivory: 99 and 44/100 Percent Pure."
"*National Enquirer:* Inquiring Minds Want to Know."
"Perdue: It Takes a Tough Man to Make a Tender Chicken."
"Bounty: The Quicker Picker-Upper."
"Let Your Fingers Do the Walking Through the Yellow Pages"
"A Diamond Is Forever."
"*Rocky* (the movie): His Whole Life Was a Million-to-One Shot."

Specific, colorful, superlative, important, memorable. They rarely make 'em like they used to. And judging by what you see at the end of print ads, commercials, and logos these days, Johnny doesn't know what he's missing and can't get it right. But you do and you can.

Fail-safe Ingredients for Your DSI Tag

When you follow the linear process for building a DSI that we'll cover in Part Two, you'll find, more often than not, you have the key ingredients for your DSI tag already prepped and waiting to be sautéed. You just take the three core message parts we always create before attempting the tag line and blend them together, making crisp, differentiating substance inevitable, as long as we stick to them. The three ingredients are (1) your Unique, Ownable Specialty, (2) your proposed DSI expression, and (3) your exclusive name. The exact proportions are left up to the cook's taste.

Here's a little example: "Roaches Check In, but They Don't Check Out," the classic DSI tag created for a product called the Black Flag Roach Motel. How did they get there?

First they took their specialty, which we'll submit was:

Safe but Strong Home Roach Control Products.

(Already we're better off than "A Passion for Excellence.")

Next, they considered their name, a combination of a great brand name and a fun but highly descriptive product name: Black Flag (which means death if anything ever did) plus Roach Motel (a totally unique and memorable name for a product that was essentially a little paper box with some poison inside and a door too tricky for the average roach to figure out how to exit). The product was easy and sanitary and minimized grossness because you never had to look at or touch the dead creatures like you do with other traps, flypaper, or sprays. But it worked like the grim roach reaper. Finally, in their tag line equation, they considered their proposed DSI, which we'll venture was something like:

Deadliest, Ick-Free Roach Trap.

Lastly, they added a bit of color and flair: "Roaches Check In, but They Don't Check Out." The line implies and pays off their exclusive name, Black Flag Roach Motel. It promises a specific, important end benefit: Roaches will be caught and eliminated. And it uses a little humor to spotlight the unique nature of the product, but not to distract from it—keeping the product the star of the show.

Let us say that the flair and the color are icing on this cake. They're a bonus derived from a talent for wordcraft that not everyone has and you shouldn't fret about if it's not your strong suit. At this point, you've earned an A+ by getting your DSI, name and Unique Ownable Specialty to where it is. Much of the time, in fact, either the articulation of your Unique Ownable Specialty or your proposed DSI expression alone can double as a great tag line themselves. Take "747: The First Jumbo Jet," for instance. That's your Unique Ownable Specialty name and a great DSI tag in one. You could've tagged the Roach

Motel with "the Easiest, Ick-Free Roach Trap" and done fine. The "Check In/Check Out" version just adds a little extra spice.

Again, clever lines like this overlap into the executional, copywriting part of expression. You're well advised to hire a good copywriter for a short project to dream up a list of lines, but be adamant—he sticks to your core message components or he doesn't get paid.

A Few Hints and Reminders

Just a few more guidelines for DSI tags:

1. The "tag lines must be short" mandate is a myth. Look at one of the best DSI tags ever, Fedex's original "When it absolutely, positively has to be there overnight," which originally put them on the map. Or Vicks Nyquil's "the nighttime, sniffling, sneezing, coughing, aching, stuffy head, fever so you can rest medicine." At fourteen words, Nyquil's is obviously an extreme. If you can say it in two or three words, say it. But what's important is that it works, not that it works in three words or less.

2. Rhyming and other tenets from eighth-grade poetry class are good. Some people stick their noses up at rhyming. Tell that to William Shakespeare, Dr. Seuss, or any bard who's defined the culture or been around for five hundred years. Rhyming is a musical memory trick that's as old as time. Alliteration, consonance, and other simple poetry devices add up to smooth, satisfying feelings to the ear and tongue. People love them.

We should all be so lucky to come up with a DSI tag like "takes a licking and keeps on ticking" or "the whole TV scene in one magazine."

3. Putting your brand name in the DSI tag is not always required. It's a case-by-case judgment, based on the context and structure of the line. "Join the Navy and see the world" is a natural to include the brand name. "Please don't squeeze the Charmin" is another one. "It's not TV, it's HBO," is a third. But

VISA doesn't require it. The line is simply locked under the logo: *"It's everywhere you want to be."*

4. Remember, a successful DSI tag does *not* always have to spell out the entire DSI in every instance; it just has to do its part to optimize the DSI. This goes to the principle of knowing where and when you're lighting the five-point DSI star so you can design the points accordingly. When you've hit your DSI with the sound of your name at point 1 of the star ("DieHard Batteries"), you don't need to follow with "the batteries that don't die out on you." In that particular case, you'd be redundant instead of moving the ball forward. Instead, you'll add more value and enrich the DSI further with a suggestion of benefit that deepens the DSI idea, making it even more unique and memorable—something like "DieHard batteries: never be stranded again."

On the other hand, if you've gone through point 1 (your name) and point 2 (your Unique Ownable Specialty) and you still haven't illuminated your DSI; then go for a complete DSI summation in the tag line. The most famous of all times is M&M's Chocolate Candies' "the milk chocolate melts in your mouth, not in your hand."

All in all, when it comes time to find your tag line, it's nice to be Shakespeare but you don't have to be. You'll get 95 percent of the way there by following the proprietary guideposts of your DSI, your specialty, and your name. And that's 95 percent better than "passionately inspired to achieve inspiration."

Now what if you're at point 3 of the star, you've got your DSI tag, but your gut says you need another hundred or so goose bumps to make your DSI sing. Is there another arrow we can pull out of the quiver? Let's go to point 4 of the star: the key visual.

CHAPTER 11

DSI Star Point 4:
Key Visuals

A landmark three-year study by the Mahesh Brand Institute, certi-
fied by the Franklin Mint, has found conclusively that "A picture is
worth only 937 words." However, that's still a lot of words.

Guru Mahatma Mahareshi "Mahesh" Goldberg

Seeing is believing. That's why point 4 of the DSI star be-
longs to *the key visual*. We're not talking here about logos, let-
terhead, color palette, "look and feel," or even product or
package graphic designs. That's the role of visual "identity,"
which is used to give us brand consistency across the whole
enterprise over time. Visual identity is like the Army's uniform
versus the Navy's uniform.

A key visual, on the other hand, is a basic tool for DSI building, defined as that one "picture worth a thousand (or so)
words" that can deliver a DSI slam dunk when you are lucky
enough, clever enough or dogged enough, to capture one.

A key visual is an indelible snapshot that demonstrates both
performance and proof—essentially your whole DSI—in a
single flash. It's a complete selling vision that needs no words:

The rifle bullet blasting through the Master Lock
The handprint on the Tempur-Pedic Foam Mattress
The drinking straw in the Tropicana Orange

The Marlboro cowboy

The Crazy Glue guy stuck to the goal post by the top of his helmet

The Boston Whaler sawed-in-half fiberglass boat, each half being rowed by a smiling kid

The silhouette of the tomato juice glass scooped out of the center of the red tomato on the Campbell's Tomato Juice cans

The frying egg from the Partnership for a Drug Free America ("This is your brain on drugs.")

The ATT Wireless (now Cingular) visual of the five full reception bars.

A minute ago, you may have noticed three qualifiers ("lucky," "clever," and "dogged") and inferred that we're downplaying your chances of creating this part of DSI messaging on your own.

We are. Of all the points of the DSI star, a powerful key visual can be the most elusive, least possible to predict in advance, and most dependent on a fortuitous moment of creative inspiration than any of the others. The fact is, not every product lends itself to a dramatic visual demo or symbol. Intangibles like accounting services for one thing. So while creating a DSI does require verbal expression—an articulated specialty, an exclusive name, and a pithy, proposed DSI, all essentially made out of words—you don't always get the chance to shoot a high-powered rifle bullet through your pasta sauce. You can't always count on having a key visual expression.

The other reason we qualify this aspect of the DSI is that great visual branding thinkers—graphic artists who are also salespeople at heart—are a rare breed, indeed. Whether you're one or not, you certainly can have a moment of brilliance or luck, however. The Boston Whaler boat sawed in half could just as easily have been the quality control manager's idea as an ad agency's. But like most of us, if you suspect there's a great key visual in your product waiting to come out, your surest path may be to seek the services of a professional visual thinker at an agency or a design studio whose mind has been wired to think this way since birth.

So what's our recommendation? Swing for the fences and go for it anyway! Any visual thinking you do will move the ball forward, expand your thinking—and if you happen to hit on the right one, eureka! We just want you to know that if you strike out, or don't even get up to bat because your product doesn't play ball—not to worry. You'll still be able to develop a great, successful Dominant Selling Idea based on the other four points of the star.

Key Ingredients for Key Visuals

The genesis of the modern key visual can be found in what the Brand Titans dubbed a "torture test" and classically trained salespeople would call "showmanship." These are quick, dramatic demos that simply say, "If the product can do *this* or clean *this* or survive *this* test before your very eyes, imagine what it'll do for you at home."

Torture tests and showmanship were refined to a fine art during the era of the gadget pitchmen in carnivals and traveling shows, and were later recreated on early TV with magic mops and slicer-dicers.

One of our favorite supershowmanship stories was about the original safety-glass salesman who would simply walk up to the buyer's desk without a word, put down a six-inch piece of safety glass, pull out a ball-peen hammer, and swing. The buyer would jump back—but of course the glass wouldn't shatter. The salesman would then pull out his order book and say, "How much do you need?" Unforgettable key visual. Sale closed.

The Master Lock rifle shot is probably the world's most famous torture test.

But great key visuals are not confined to torture tests alone. They can also be dramatic visual metaphors that suggest a superlative, important, and memorable idea of value. The baby in the Michelin tire is a key visual metaphor. So is the Marlboro cowboy, Prudential's Rock of Gibraltar, and the famous Rolling Stones' tongue.

None of these key visuals is an abstract symbol; each is a multidimensional selling idea. The Michelin baby sells us the promise of ultimate safety for our loved ones, a group that includes us. The tongue sells Mick Jagger's one-of-a-kind voice, songs, and irreverent personality. The Jolly Green Giant sells us canned vegetables we can trust to have a big, fresh, green taste. Torture tests like the "Hefty Bag stre-e-e-e-tching when others break" speak for themselves.

Dreaming Up Your Own

Like any DSI-related component—whether it be a great name, unique specialty, or DSI tag—the basic strategy to use for guidance is the DSI parts you've already come up with, parts you will have already established in the DSI creative process before attempting a key visual or dramatic demo.

For example, if your proposed DSI for Tropicana was "Juice so fresh, it's like drinking an orange," you can see where the inspiration for a drinking straw stuck directly into an orange might come from.

Key visuals are meant to be fun, dramatic, surprising, and whimsical. So let your imagination run free when brainstorming them. There's nothing to lose—especially when creating torture tests. Think of the worst-case scenario that your product can handle—even if it's a little farfetched. For example, let's say your product is a really terrific car wax. What's the worst, most impossibly filthy car situation your wax could be asked to remedy? How about a car in the junkyard? One of our all-time favorites was an early direct-response TV commercial for a miracle car wax that was so effective, it could make the finish on a junkyard car look like new. They picked a car in a pile of wrecks and polished it to a fine shine in minutes. It was a miracle. Imagine what it could do for your car. The key visual that came out of all this was a still shot of a hand buffing a junk car's hood, with the polished part looking like new.

Prudential wanted to set itself apart as the brand consumers think of first when seeking a rock-solid insurance company. So they simply found the world's biggest, most famous rock (the Rock of Gibraltar) and used it as their key visual. Can't be any more straight ahead than that. The milk industry wanted to instill the idea that a kid's drink whose unique end benefit was that it could give you a white mustache when you were aged six was something else: a natural, tasty drink endorsed by adult celebrities who reminded us that good nutrition can also come with a kid's sense of fun. They simply put white mustaches on everyone from Michael Jordan to Cindy Crawford and created one of the most famous key visuals ever.

There's no formula for creating key visuals other than this: focus on your DSI core, make all the logical and not so logical connections you can, and don't be afraid to be zany, dramatic, and fun. You, your colleagues, and in-laws are guaranteed to think of demos, torture tests, and apt metaphors. Follow your thinking all the way through and imagine yourself taking snapshots of the results, looking for the one defining shot that captures the moment of truth.

Remember the shot of the Marines raising the flag on Iwo Jima? America's key visual for all of World War II was taken by a dogged, professional photographer who knew exactly what he was looking for . . . and then got lucky.

CHAPTER 12

DSI Start Point 5: DSI-Level Performance— Making It Tangible

Once upon a time, there was a new professional daredevil. He read a book and decided to become his own brand. He got a great name, Daytona Devilish. He got a great specialty, "Rush Hour Rocket Man." He got a DSI tag and a key visual. He got a surplus Russian cruise missile welded onto his Corolla. Then he invited Las Vegas to watch him jump thirty-three flaming tour buses to beat a cop who was chasing him up the breakdown lane. The countdown began. The crowds held their breath. The Corolla blasted off. Daytona soared majestically over the roofs of sixteen buses and through the baggage compartments of seventeen buses. This is why there are no Daytona Devilish toys, TV shows, or fried chicken restaurants today.

Guru Mahatma Mahareshi "Mahesh" Goldberg

In the end, it all comes down to this. Old-fashioned horse sense—what your father told you, and his father told him, and they were right:

You either perform or you don't. Your DSI is either made tangible for the customer, or it's not. You function as promised and you make someone's life or job better, or no manner of brand expression can save you. When someone trusts you with his time and money, and you punt, the DSI you proffered is erased; replaced by a skull and bones or, equally damning, a blank void. As a matter of fact, the irony is that nothing kills a brand faster than great DSI messaging for a bad product because you combine accelerated trial and high anticipation with high disappointment, leading to anger and betrayal. In our language, that spells *dead*.

So we'll assume that going into the branding process, your product is fundamentally sound, efficacious and lives up to the universal contract of value between buyer and seller. If not, your needs are more elemental than a great DSI.

Point Five Is About Performance, Plus

Point 5 of the star is about something beyond the baseline performance expectations that customers have for all specialties. DSI-level performance means the physical differences in product and performance we can add to elevate the customer's experience of us beyond the norm—the differences that highlight, express, and make tangible our DSI during the actual physical experience of our brand. In many cases, these physical differences define the brand and lock in its DSI more indelibly than any of the other four points of the star.

You come to a Cold Stone Creamery ice cream shop for the first time, not because you've seen any advertising, but because you've heard by word of mouth. When you walk in, you walk into a DSI—you see unexpected, appealing product differences all around that are thematically consistent and uniquely Cold Stone. These are differences on top of the quality benchmarks for any ice cream store: clean, bright surroundings, ice cream on display, and friendly kids behind the counter. These are Cold Stone bonuses: only a few "base" flavors displayed, next to a thousand mix-ins, some familiar like crushed Health Bars and some really fun and original like chopped-up apple pies and cheese cake crusts. Right away it's different. As you get close to the counter, you see the big frozen stone where all the mixing's done. Instead of being bored in line, you get to watch the outrageous flavors get created fresh by skilled employees for the folks in front of you, and you get to see if theirs is better than yours or really disgusting. The décor is full of whacky flavor suggestions and ice cream photos. The staff refer to themselves as ice cream consultants. There is no walking out of Cold Stone without perceiving a wonderful, unique brand experience that you or anyone else can articulate enthusiastically to the uninitiated whom you'll inevitably tell, "What, you've never been to Cold Stone? It's this ice cream place where they mix any flavor of ice cream you want on a frozen counter, right in front of you." That's a DSI installed while you're on the premises, then reinforced whenever you think of Cold Stone afterward. The performance in this case is not just the unusual ice cream—it's the whole ice cream store experience you get at Cold Stone that's like a little vacation in the middle of your day. You can't separate the ice cream from the mixing process from the "packaging"—i.e., the visual décor—from the counter help who sing "thank you" every time a tip is given. It's product and performance rolled into one.

You test drive a Jaguar. You walk around the car and savor every famous angle. You listen to the perfect, muted thump of the closing door, smell the English leather, and take in the unique Jaguar interior—the delicate wooden shifter, the classic analogue instruments, the driver's cockpit that's more comfortably refined than the heavy German power wagons you've driven before. You feel the acceleration and the sweet handling in turns you take just a little faster than normal. You're having a DSI-level brand experience, checking the box in your brain next to the brand promise which says, "Real." If after all the hype, it drove like an old Buick Skylark, Jaguar's DSI in your head would be instantly, and irrevocably, kaput.

Beyond Retail, Restaurants, Hotels, and Other High-Touch Products

When you're devising specific DSI-level differences for your product, you try to bring performance into alignment with your DSI at every customer "touch point"—that is, every interaction a customer can have with you regardless of time or place. That's because every interaction is an opportunity to make your brand more tangible on some level. This is that process we call *Total Consistent Alignment (TCA)* in the overall branding process.

Now obviously, some businesses are inherently more conducive to customer touch than others. Retail stores like Cold Stone, restaurants, hotels, and other public service establishments have a product that customers literally enter and surround themselves with. Starbucks can reinforce a unique brand experience a hundred different ways before you even taste the coffee. If you manufacture canned tomato juice, on the other hand, you're situation's at the opposite end of the spectrum. Brand experience is confined to seeing and holding your package and drinking the juice. Not every product is born with thousands of options when it comes to point 5.

Yet just by thinking in DSI-level terms, options will always present themselves. It's surprising how much Total Consistent Alignment you can devise when you follow your DSI logically through to every nook and cranny of your customers' experience, then adjust your product and performance to match.

HealthMarket was a revolutionary kind of health insurance company that could significantly lower premiums for small-business people, without stripping benefits. The problem was, management was great at designing health plans, but not good at making the rules simple to understand. Plan members were making mistakes, receiving extra charges that seemed unfair, and getting angry. The brand was in danger of an unrecoverable condition—mistrust reaching critical mass. HealthMarket needed a new DSI—then needed to make it believable in a hurry with specific performance changes that members could see, hear, and touch. Their new proposed DSI was "the only affordable health plan that gives you control." The company promised it would become more accessible and flexible with personal choice than the old-fashioned insurance companies were. And in return for customers getting more involved and making better health choices, they'd provide convenient services to make it easy and keep premiums down.

Then HealthMarket set out to make it real and tangible at every touch point. They did small things like attaching little red "activation" stickers on every new membership card, inviting new members to call for a personal orientation. They changed the name of their customer service reps to "personal assistants"—and empowered them to be truly that—to go above and beyond the limits of conventional customer service and get directly involved as member advocates. They rewrote their user guides in simple, everyday English, eliminating insurance speak. They gave each member a personal health savings account to spend any way they wanted for preventive care. HealthMarket simplified its rules in every way possible, making material product adjustments to minimize the chances of member mistakes. They even created a little dog mascot who appeared as a company spokesman—putting a disarming, welcoming face on health insurance that consumers had never seen before. As HealthMarket walked this walk, their talk resonated, and their new DSI took hold—not only on the outside with expanded sales and renewals, but, just as importantly, on the inside, by refreshing the whole company's sense of mission.

Creating Touch Points from Scratch

In HealthMarket's case, they scoured their business for more touch points and maximized Total Consistent Alignment with what they had. Another practical alternative when your brand is tangibility challenged is to develop peripheral experiences from scratch that can be attached to your brand, creating touch points by association. For example, more and more brands are creating "communities" and events where like-minded and loyal customers get together in person and online to share brand living experiences. There are sponsored Harley Davidson, Ducati, and BMW events and clubs, Barcardi beach parties and Hawaiian tan bikini contests. Yes, these for the most part are downstream brand-building tactics that go beyond the scope of where we are now in building the DSI star. But the underlying concept is based on solid DSI thinking, namely, to show your DSI performing in the real world, setting your brand experience apart in superlative, important, and memorable ways.

Thinking in DSI

That last point about "solid DSI thinking" is the crux of everything we seek to accomplish here at DSI University and our footbridge to the eight-week DSI process. The goal of an enlightened education is not to teach students how to recite facts and figures; it's to teach them how to analyze, how to judge, how to tell right from wrong, *how to think*. Because in the immortal words of the old Peace Corps commercials in the '60s, "Give a man a bag of corn and you feed him for a day. Teach him to plant a field of corn and you feed him for a lifetime." Or something like that.

DSI is a way of thinking, not an action or a step or set of rules. It's a branding state of mind.

Look back at the five-point star. Put yourself back on the DSI tour. Make brands stand up to the ultimate DSI messaging test. Print our favorite acronym (SIBMT) backwards on your forehead. In all the fog and confusion, do you now see those headlights on the DSI locomotives coming right at you? Do you have the urge to put your brand on that train?

Everything up to now has been about getting you to this way of thinking. It will guide you at every branding step, as long as you hold it out in front of you and keep reaching for it, always.

Now all aboard. Next stop: "Eight weeks to your Dominant Selling Idea."

PART TWO

Doing

Eight Weeks to Your DSI

The Next Eight Weeks

Now that you know why the AFLAC duck is not a Dominant Selling Idea, we're ready to begin.

Guru Mahatma Mahareshi "Mahesh" Goldberg

Friends, in spite of what some pundits, consultants, and aficionados may tell you, it does not take six months of exploratories to reveal the one Dominant Selling Idea for your brand. We've been doing this now for over twenty-five years at companies ranging from global packaged goods giants to Internet startups. And we can tell you this:

> *Once you've arrived at the DSI mind-set—the point where you can stand up at an advertising luncheon in New York and inform them that the AFLAC duck is not a Dominant Selling Idea because it's neither Superlative, Important, nor Believable—it's merely Memorable like the dancing bear on the rooftop—causing The Wall Street Journal to admit that after five years, no one knows what they're supposed to buy, that is—once you've reached the DSI understanding you have now:*

It takes about eight weeks to come up with your own. Eight weeks to arrive at what we've called your *proposed DSI*, the #1 specialty attached to your name that you can transfer into other people's heads through consistent performance, messaging, and ongoing refinement of the DSI star.

If you can't find your DSI in eight weeks, it's not because you lack the capability or desire; it's because something else is seriously wrong with your product, your specialty, your credibility, your reputation or conduct within the industry—something that no words or idea medicine can fix. In fact, great words and stories only make such problems more glaring and transparent, hastening the departure of the wheels from your bus.

Our assumption is that you have something to brand that you'd sell to your seventh-grade teacher, your priest, or your mother-in-law with confidence and enthusiasm—a worthy, fairly priced product or service and a company of which you are proud. A product that's not necessarily perfect because none are. Just one that you love. That single, simple emotion is the chief stuff that people have transmuted into great DSIs for thousands of years.

We also assume that, like all the world's top businesspeople including ourselves, you have attention deficit disorder. For that reason, you'll find this next section more prescriptive, short, and direct by design than what's come before. Part One of this book is solely intended to raise your overall intuition to DSI level, so that even if you fail to read another page, you'll be way ahead of where you started. You'll know a real selling brand when you see one, know the basic steps to attain yours, and know how to track what you're getting from your branding effort or any agency you hire to help.

Part Two of this book, on the other hand, is a specific primer for anyone who wants to do it for themselves, right now. It's like any instruction manual. You hold it open and follow the directions.

How Far Can You Really Get by the End of Week Eight?

Stunningly far. Paradigm shiftingly far. You'll have entered the gates of the real brand Promised Land because you will have uncovered a #1 specialty that is Superlative, Important, and Believable and can be made Memorable and Tangible. The first three of those selling ingredients set up your proposed DSI, which means you have correctly "positioned" your brand and can articulate it exactly. This alone is a huge, life-changing milestone for any company and brand. You've nailed your core concept.

The last two ingredients, Memorable and Tangible, make it possible for your DSI to penetrate and stick in customers' heads, long term. Memorable and Tangible result from completing your DSI's expression—the five-point DSI star—and executing it for the rest of your life. Since decision flow varies widely in organizations as do creative resources, no one can anticipate the exact amount of time it will take you to agree on a final list of names, choose your favorite tag lines, dream up a key visual, or implement the number of TCA changes you'll choose to make your DSI perform as promised. Only you and your colleagues can manage that.

Some brands have actually achieved all five points of the DSI star in eight weeks. We've seen it and done it, so it's possible. And given the extent that you'll be immersed and cogitating on pure brand issues, it's not uncommon to have the perfect name or DSI tag materialize on its own during your research and discovery interviews. But it's really rare to complete the whole DSI star in this time frame and there's seldom a real business need to push such a fast track, any more than you need to make a toddler walk at eight months versus ten. She'll walk for sure, so long as you follow the loving process of nurturing and encouragement. You'll get to your five-point star by following the process, too.

Time Line for the Next Eight Weeks

The night before you begin, reread all seventeen of the Granite Pages. We mean it. They are the guiding fundamentals and will prime your pump for the task at hand.

The rest of the time looks like this, give or take a few days on either side:

Week 1   Plan and start your basic market research and discovery (R&D): Questions, objectives, and personal interviews.

Week 2   Conduct R&D interviews.

Week 3   Complete R&D interviews and consolidate your learnings.

Week 4   Choose three potential Unique Ownable Specialties.
Articulate key "reasons why."
Write specialty statements for top three candidates.
Test the specialty statements.

Week 5   Choose your #1 specialty. Finalize your specialty statement.
Reduce it to a proposed DSI.

Week 6   Formulate and test a brand story narrative.

Weeks 7 and 8   Inventory core elements status and plan remaining points of DSI star as needed: naming strategy, DSI tag development, key visual, and Total Consistent Alignment (TCA). Begin execution of all remaining points based on your DSI.

Who's Really Going to Do This—You? A Subordinate? An Agency?

We're going to show you the methods we use every day—the basic process that we do personally as brand consultants. But before we did this for others, we did it successfully for our own companies as employees and entrepreneurs. In other words, there's no rule that says you can't do any piece of this process yourself if you have the desire and a little DSI discipline. We'll present it; you'll decide how much or little you want to entrust to others. The only rule is that you be closely involved, follow your new intuition, and ask the various DSI test questions every step of the way. And bear in mind that someone had better be performing every one of these steps for your brand to reach its DSI. If you hear excuses or substitutes or spurious thinking, get different help.

Some senior executives don't imagine themselves asking direct, candid questions of customers, employees, or other stakeholders, feeling that it's inappropriate or awkward. But the ones who do learn invaluable insights that only come from being face to face and intimately involved. Others feel insecure in "creative" sessions. But those who dive in nearly always surprise themselves. A great idea can come from anywhere. Look at how many great scientific discoveries happened because someone dropped a stale piece of cheese from his sandwich into the petri dish by accident. The genius was simply that they stopped, took notice, kept an open mind—and didn't let the moment pass them by.

If You're a Big Company

Eight weeks is how long it takes to get from here to your proposed DSI in normal traffic. Whether you're a $25 billion global corporation or a $250,000 a year startup, a Dominant Selling Idea is no more or less complex; the real distance between you and truth is no more convoluted. But let's not kid ourselves. Big companies have "logistical" issues smaller companies don't have—like layered organizations, multiple geographies, fiefdoms, and Politics with a capital P. In any eight-week time period, you've got to hit some traffic congestion somewhere, which will most likely slow you down. Instead of three weeks for the research-and-discovery interview process, it might take four to get on the schedules of everyone you want to see. If certain parties insist on more comprehensive modes of concept or copy testing or your chief legal counsel is on vacation, you add a few more days. These are the kinds of process extenders we also can't predict for you. To our amazement, we once saw a case where it took an entire year to perform the most expensive, scientifically researched, consultant-laden exploratory of a corporate brand identity imaginable—the sum total of which yielded, we're not kidding, a PowerPoint presentation with a lot of statistical data and a change in the angle of a key logo element by fifteen degrees. (Not our client.)

But let's be absolutely clear on this—a big company that wants to clear the road and find its Dominant Selling Idea in eight weeks, can.

Just follow the plan.

Now start rereading those Granite Pages. Turn to the following chapter when done.

CHAPTER 13

The Keys to the Safe:
Weeks 1 to 3

The legendary sales manager for the Tibetan Recurring Life &
Casualty Insurance Co. said to me, "A great salesman's secret is the
opposite of what you think. He doesn't want to talk—he wants you
to talk. He keeps asking you questions and listening to your needs
and wishes. He waits until you've given him the answers. Then he
tells you exactly what you want to hear."

Guru Mahatma Mahareshi "Mahesh" Goldberg

Ask and Ye Shall Receive

The part of the process that Johnny always talks about *but
never does* is now upon us—the most important part: the part
that involves formulating a few commonsense questions, then
going outside the compound, even for a day or two, to meet
real stakeholders in person, one on one. That means actual
customers, prospects, people who saw your product but didn't
buy, competitors' employees or exemployees, and maybe an
analyst or two. No less important, it includes stepping outside
your office and talking with your employees—especially your
customer service reps and salespeople in the field. In most
companies, people pay lip service to this step—yet it is where
you get 90 to 95 percent of the answers you're looking for.
Literally.

If you appear trustworthy and ask people the right questions, then listen to what they say and watch what they say
with their body and facial expressions, people will hand you

the keys to the safe. That is, they will tell you, step by step, exactly what they need to be sold and how to sell them. They will tell you what really matters most that no one else is providing. They'll tell you what your brand really is (what they think you stand for), which is the direct, physical result of their good or lousy experiences with your product and your company, not your advertising campaign, no matter how many quacking ducks you have. Likewise, they'll tell you what your specialty actually is so you can infer what specialty you could or should be in if you're not #1 in your current specialty, now. They'll tell you your competitors' specialties, their DSIs (if any), and what their strengths and vulnerabilities are. They will tell you because people love to talk to those who really want to listen and they love to feel they're helping. They will provide you with great selling language, colorful metaphors, and examples, all the creative material you need. Free.

Take notes and make sure you collect it all. Then we guarantee the following: You will ALWAYS be surprised by something. You will learn simple things and see truths you can't believe you missed.

You will be amazed at the likelihood that someone you never expected, without realizing it, simply lays your big idea in your lap. Amazed, that is, if you open yourself up enough to see it. Sometimes, you'll even walk away with a killer tag line or a new name that somebody just hands you.

Bottom line, your solution is delivered by your questions, as any good detective knows. If you do it right, you'll get 90 percent or more toward where you want to go in the first two to three weeks—during the research-and-discovery (R&D) phase.

R&D Phase, Step by Step

Here's the plan for each step of the R&D phase, which we'll go over in detail in the following pages. It will take about a day to plan, one to three days to set up appointments, and a week and a half to two weeks to execute—primarily by conducting face-to-face meetings and making phone calls when personal meetings are impossible. These are the simple steps:

1. Decide on the specific objectives for your questions. What exactly do you want to know?
2. List the people who can tell you what you want to know.
3. Prepare your list of big questions.
4. Smile and dial to schedule face-to-face meetings whenever possible.
5. Interview, using the "six honest serving men" and "question strings."
6. Listen with your eyes, ears, arms, legs, and torso.
7. Narrow your questions as you get closer to the real answers.
8. Afterward, spread out your Halloween candy, and see what you've got.

Before we go over each step, let's clarify a few points with a quick "Question and Answer":

Q: *How many people do we need to talk to?*
A: In our own experience, confirmed by professional research people we've known over the years, ten to twelve people is the rule of thumb for any related group of "A" people. By "A" people, we mean corporate management, sales and marketing, customers and prospects, IT department, designers, competitors—whoever matters most in your business process. That's enough to see trends, get variety, and avoid duplication. But it's always a judgment call based on your time, resources, and size of the universe. The reality of schedules, time, and patience being what it is, you'll be doing superbly if you speak to anywhere from twenty to twenty-five people total in the entire R&D process. That might mean four salespeople because that's the entire sales force, ten customers because that's the total you could reach, one analyst, and eleven inside managers

and staff, for example. You'll be able to tell that you've seen and heard enough when the answers start to jell.

Q: *Can't I just do one focus group and kill twelve birds with one stone?*
A: We'll let the Guru answer this one:
 "No freakin' way, Jose Mubarik."

Thank you, Guru. You can't cut this corner with focus groups if you want the answers to your future. You've got to do one-on-ones. Here's why:

We don't like Focus Groups.

In aggregate, focus groups do more harm to more marketing programs than they do good because of all the executives they lead down the wrong paths. Focus groups generate twisted, group psychological dynamics that will nearly always skew the attitudes, answers, and overall candor of people in the room. Most people, after all, don't purchase products in gangs of ten. What happens is that one or two natural influencers quickly emerge who consciously or unconsciously affect the perspectives of everyone at the table. Following their natural inclination to please, people start impressing each other, embellishing stories, and selecting memories. When one person says something golden, you can't zero in the way you need to because you have to accommodate the commentary and interruptions of all the others.

There are famous stories of focus group people who describe their habitual behavior with certain products in excruciating detail—then are secretly filmed afterward doing the exact opposite.

You must have the opportunity for personal rapport building, spontaneous questioning, and confidentiality that only comes with one-on-ones.

Focus groups can be worthwhile on a superficial level when

you want to "disaster check" reactions to an idea or an advertising campaign. They are never the place to search for original truth.

Q: *Why in person? Can't it at least be over the phone?*
A: You'll never be able to see everyone face to face, so some phone calls will have to do. But there is no substitute for face-to-face meetings. Spend the money and take the time if you possibly can. As any professional salesperson will tell you, it's not new-age pabulum but a fact that people communicate on six or seven levels in every conversation—words being only one level. There are windows to their souls in their posture, their facial expressions, their word cadence, their pitch, their hand gestures, their breathing—not to mention their eyes themselves. Since all humans communicate this way, we're all unconscious masters of this language, even though we may not realize it. It speaks to us in the form of intuition, feelings, "chemistry," unspoken trust or distrust—the subtext of conversations where we know people are saying one thing (even truthfully) but we know they're meaning another.

Needless to say, you need to be within a few feet of someone to communicate in all these critical dimensions—if you want the maximum shot at truth, that is.

1. Our Objective: Where Are We?

Before we can go anywhere, we've got to know exactly where we are today both from our own perspective and from the market's perspective. So our first job is to collect and catalog reality by listening to key stakeholders inside and outside the company in their own unscripted words.

On a macro level, you're listening for patterns, themes, and intelligence that portend reality about the specialty, the competition, the market opportunity, and the unique capacities that can coalesce into a real selling brand. Hearing all the ways opinions diverge is as important as hearing the ones that converge.

On a micro level, you're listening for golden nuggets of language, expression, and metaphors that will go into your palette later on when you paint your picture of the Dominant Selling Idea. Take careful notes. You'll be amazed at how often a throwaway phrase from a junior customer service manager, talking about something else, turns out to be a piece of creative inspiration.

On a practical level, you'll be listening for them to tell you:

- What's the company's real specialty?
- How does the company articulate its specialty now?
- Where does it rank in sales, product quality, and leadership status in its specialty?
- What's most important to customers when they buy? Removal of what pain? Improvement of what aspect? What attributes? What end benefits?
- Where's the Sweet Spot for the specialty's attributes, that is, where is the dividing line between meaningful, measurable differentiation and ungraspable hyperbole in the customer's mind?
- What sets the company apart? What does it do that nobody else does, and how important is that to the market?
- What are its most serious weaknesses?
- What are the company's values?
- Who's the competition? What are they famous for?
- What does the competition do better? Does the market know it?
- In a head-to-head pitch, why does the company win? Why does it lose?
- What's the biggest thing customers wish they had more of that they don't get now from any company?
- What will make this company #1 in its specialty? Or is there a more advantageous specialty for this company to compete in and dominate?

- What will the industry look like in three years? Who will dominate and why?
- Where will this company be in three years?
- Does the market understand this company? What should they know that they don't know today?

If some of the above seem obvious, they are! All the more reason why you should ask them. The answers to some of the simplest questions will enlighten you. We're after the fundamentals, don't forget.

There isn't a question above that can't be asked of those outside as well as inside the company. Obviously, you won't always get outsiders to answer—but listen up when they do. When you can get an outsider to opine about your current specialty, your greatest strengths, your greatest weaknesses, your status versus the competition, unexploited opportunities, or your internal company values, take extragood notes.

2. Who You Should Talk To

Make a list divided by Inside and Outside.

Inside the Company

You'll want to talk to the key influencers, decision makers, and representatives of the business's vital organs. That means besides the obvious "C"-level people (CEO, COO, chief marketing officer, head of sales, etc.), you may want to zero in on the VP of customer service and several customer service reps if the organization is call-center–oriented, IT people and programmers if you're in software, and brand managers if you're in packaged goods.

Seek Out the Salespeople

Salespeople in virtually any business are vital to you because they bridge the Inside and Outside every day. They are the closest thing to interviewing real customers and prospects, especially when real customers are difficult to corral, because salespeople make their livelihood by listening and responding to real customers' comments and complaints each day. They also spend their time trying to outdo the competition, which generally tunes them in to competitors' specialties as well. Good salespeople as a group are often the most practical thinkers in the organization because results are the only thing they're compensated for—and results come consistently from what works, not from what theoretically works.

The goal is to identify at least fifteen to twenty people who represent the heart and mind of the company from top to bottom—from the corporate sky boxes down to the playing field. Every level has their own perspective. Your best answers may come from anyplace. You can do four to six interviews a day, averaging about an hour each. The good news is they're captive and you can find them so you can usually do them all in person by setting aside two to three solid days with a little advance notice.

Interview with a Partner When You Can

It's ideal to conduct your interviews with a second person listening and taking notes along with you. A second person will always observe and hear things you don't or think of the question you missed. Your combined notes will be richer.

Just remember to establish going in who's the "lead questioner" and who's the "colleague" in each interview, so that you don't step on each other, impede the spontaneity of the conversation, and possibly confuse the person being interviewed.

Outside the Company

Make it your goal to talk to at least the same number of people outside as you talk to inside. You may have industry pros on the inside who are as knowledgeable as anyone about industry trends, the competition, and the market. But outside is where the buck stops on brand reality. When possible, you want to talk to

Current customers
Past customers—those who've left
Prospects you've pitched to and lost
Target group, unpitched
Competitors—job recruits, exemployees, current employees
Industry observers
  Analysts
  Press—editors and reporters
  Newsletter writers
  Government regulators
  Investors

You won't be able to contact every one on this list. That's why current customers are your easiest, most productive outside starting point. Current customers have usually been former customers of competitors, are currently fielding calls for competitive presentations, and attend trade shows where they learn a lot about the industry they'll share with you.

Seeing lapsed customers, those you've pitched and lost, and employees of competitors is no doubt a trickier endeavor. Make it your goal to contact as many as you can in this group. Interviews "from the dark side" can be worth their weight in gold.

3. The Big Questions

Have you ever heard the old saw that there are only six universal plots in all literature, so that every single work of fiction is just a variation on those six? Well, in DSI R&D, there are a group of universal questions you should ask everybody plus a few discretionary ones if you have time. From the answers you get, you can nearly always construct the plot you're after.

Word them however you like, as long as they're direct and focused. You'll rarely have time to ask them all so don't pressure yourself. You can combine them. If you get through eight to ten and can hold the subject for an hour, you're doing great.

Twelve Eternal Internal Questions

Ask these of everyone from the CEO to the route drivers:

1. Explain what part of the industry you're in and what group of customers you serve. Does this business specialty have a name?
2. Where do you rank in this specialty: one, two, or three?
3. Why does the world need your company? What do customers want most?
4. What do you do for people that nobody else does? How important is it to your customers? Do you stand for that *by name* in your customers' minds? Does anybody?
5. What's your "unsung" ability—the #1 thing the market needs to know about your company they don't know now?
6. Tell me your value proposition:
   "We're the #1 choice for _____ and _____, so you can _____ and _____. That's because we have _____."
7. What worries you about your company? What keeps you up at night?
8. What about your company makes you most proud?
9. Who are your competitors? What are they famous for, if anything?
10. Why do you win and why do you lose in head-to-head competition?
11. Does your company have a mission or set of values? What is it?
12. If we asked five customers or prospects, what would they say your company stands for?

Ten Eternal External Questions

When you talk to people on the outside, you want to ask nearly the same set of questions, not only to get a fumes-free perspective because all of us breathe our own fumes, but to take the disparity between what your company thinks about itself and what the world outside thinks, and lay it out in the light of day.

Ask, from their point of view:

1. What is your business specialty? Who are your customers?
2. Where do you rank in this specialty: one, two, or three?
3. If you're not #1 in your specialty, who's #1 and why?
4. When people hear your company's name, what main idea comes to mind . . . something you do or stand for? What are you famous for, if anything?
5. What do customers want or need most from companies in this specialty?
6. List the main competitors. Are any of them famous for anything?
7. What does your company do that makes it unique from competitors?
8. What's your stated value proposition in a pitch? For example,
   "We're the #1 choice for _____ and _____, so you can _____ and _____ because we have _____."
9. Is there an unaddressed pain point or need in the market your company could focus on to gain competitive advantage?
10. Do they trust your company more, less, or equally to its competitors?

Bonus Questions

If this company was a Buick hub cap, what wheel would it be on?

Just wanted to see if you're awake. The fact is, every company is different and unique in some way, so you'll invariably have specific questions you want to ask each company that are one of a kind—even random. If something intrigues you, ask it—even if the person you're asking (or your partner sitting next to you) isn't sure why. Sometimes it occurs to you on the spot because an answer points you there. Trust your instincts. Be flexible. Truth can come from anywhere.

Here are some examples:

1. Describe a day in the life of your average sales rep.
2. Why do so many of your customer service agents quit?
3. Do you use your own product?
4. What should the tag line for the company really be?
5. What's the #1 secret you don't ever want your competitors to know?
6. Do employees have fun at the Christmas party?

Remember, ask and ye shall receive.

Smiling and Dialing
Pick up the phone. Don't wait till after lunch. Stop procrastinating. Now.

4. How to Ask Questions

Starting from Trust
No one is going to tell you anything worth knowing, risk exposing their true feelings, or go to the heart of the matter—nor should they—if you don't have their trust. The #1 way to gain it is to be trustworthy.

Set up the ground rules at the start of the interview. Explain the importance of your mission. Let your interviewee know that your questions will be direct, and affirm that nothing is more important than their candid viewpoint, no matter how unpleasant or awkward it may be. Then, most important of all, say and mean that whatever is said in the room that can be attributable to them, stays in the room unless they give their explicit permission. Look them in the eye when you say it and ask if they understand and are comfortable with the rules. It's called "creating a container of trust."

Whether you're their peer, their boss or even their subordinate, a sincere attempt to create this container is your best hope to establish a vessel of truth.

The Six Honest Serving Men

> "There are six honest serving men, they tell me all I know. Their names are *why* and *who* and *what* and *when* and *where* and *how*."

> Anon

In grade school, those words were called the "interrogatives." According to Dale Carnegie, a titan not of brands but of common sense in dealing with people, they are the keys to asking "open" questions, the kind that return a thoughtful reply rather than a simple yes or no.

You're using your questions to facilitate a conversation, not an interrogation or a news conference where you're allowed one question, one answer. Your preset list of questions are a paved road and you're an off-road vehicle. You can swing the steering wheel and go overland anytime you see a more compelling route to your destination.

We begin asking questions with our interrogatives at the ready, responding to the replies we get with sharpening questions that shorten the distance to the real answer. We call it using question strings.

Question Strings

When people answer a question that has profound implications for them professionally, emotionally, or intellectually, they seldom get to the root of the problem—their bedrock answer—on the first try. Not because they're obfuscating. Chances are, they're just not used to diving so deep and describing what's on the bottom. They need a little coaching. When we sense that an answer is scratching the surface but not getting underneath, *question strings* can get us there. It's quite simple. Each time they respond, keep peeling back the onion with the "six honest serving men" and you'll find you can get down to basement level in two or three tries. You're asking them to keep narrowing the point by repeating, in effect, "And what's behind *that* door?" "And what's behind *that* door?" "Take me to the core."

For example

Q: *What* keeps you up at night?
A: The state regulators that are threatening a class action against us.

Q: *And how* will you be affected by that?
A: It's expensive, it's distracting and will slow sales, but I know we'll win.

Q: *And why* do you lose sleep over that?
A: What bothers me most is that it's unfair. They're not looking at all the good we do or what this company's about. They're jumping on the actions of three rogue salespeople out of a thousand who broke our rules and caused customer complaints that were picked up by a reporter in Omaha, and then the lawyers got it. We dismissed those reps the second we found out.

Q: *Who* else might be to blame, besides those three sales-people and the lawyers?
A: The buck stops with us for not managing to our values and not communicating who we are to the outside world. If people inside and outside understood exactly what we stand for, we'd get the benefit of the doubt more often with regulators and the press. We'd make better decisions because of it.

Q: *So, what* should the market know you really stand for?
A: Wait a minute! YOU'RE ASKING ABOUT OUR DSI! I knew it! I read *Why Johnny Can't Brand*! Hey, is the Guru a real person?

5. Tactical Listening

During our one-on-ones, listening matters more than for just the obvious reason. It's also our chief tactic for building trust and rapport over the entire process to ensure the veracity of the feedback.

Here's why: All human beings have a deep longing to be understood and to feel important. It's almost impossible not to like someone who treats us accordingly and when we like someone, we relax and open ourselves up to trust. When a person listens to us with real interest and intensity, it signals their desire to understand and respect us on this most fundamental level, and we respond in kind.

So it's not enough just to listen; our actions must prove it. We do it by utilizing the other six or seven levels of communication besides words that we mentioned earlier. We listen back with our eyes, our voice tone and cadence, our gestures, our facial expressions and body position—all the same communication tools we use to "speak" with.

We make direct eye contact. We lean forward to hear what they're saying. We secretly bite our lip to control our terrible habit of interrupting. We signal our respect the more we get in physical sync with them by slowing down and softening our voice if they do or vice versa; by sitting the way they sit; and by returning smiles. The unconscious impression is that this person feels "congruent" with me. It's the #1 building block of rapport.

Listening so actively has the wonderful side effect of tuning us in much more sharply to what's being communicated, making us smarter about the text and the subtext of what we're hearing. It gives us HDTV with surround sound. The contrasts are sharper, the colors are deeper, we hear the background tones. Our hunches are more frequent and on the mark.

All because of tactical listening.

What to Listen For

You are panning for gold. Listen for nuggets that inevitably appear in the sand. Along with the straight-ahead answers that will add up to important themes, you'll pick up Golden Metaphors as people reach down to describe ideas, feelings, and aspirations. The nuggets will present themselves as little sparks that tickle your imagination. Write them all down verbatim if you can. We can't tell you how many points of the DSI star first appeared as one of these little nuggets casually dropped into a conversation. Sometimes, they're ready for prime time as delivered.

For example, there was the time that a couple of entrepreneurs were trying to explain the idea for a new business venture that was going to develop online banking software. First, the prospective CEO went through a lengthy discourse about banking trends, the economics of bricks and mortar, and risks of "disintermediation." We had no idea what he wanted to sell. Then his partner tried to explain it using a series of statistics on consumer banking preferences, which showed all the major trend lines heading toward a collision at the exact point in business space they had in mind. Except we weren't getting it in *our* minds. Finally, the kid with the blue hair who was going to design the software blurted out, *"It's like having an ATM in your home."*

"Wait," we said. "Can you repeat that one more time?"

He said, "Well, yeah, you can kinda think of it as your own personal ATM machine on your PC screen. Your put in your PIN and password and you can do almost everything the teller does for you now whenever you feel like it without standing in the teller line. Or having to drive someplace in the snow."

Behold, a shimmering nugget. We picked it out of the pan. We twirled it around in our fingers. We got it.

The eventual product was indeed named *Home ATM*. It became the industry standard for easy-to-use home banking software and the basis for the company's DSI. The company was sold four and a half years after inception for $150 million.

And it was in our seventeenth interview with a multinational corporate insurance brokerage firm, a thirty-minute conversation with a district manager, that we heard this:

"I was trained as a CPA. I look at risk like any other financial component because, by definition, to be in business, all companies assume risk. My clients are ships on this sea of risk—the better I help them navigate, the more they save, the more liability they avoid, the more competitive advantage they have. That's a very positive thing. The whole world just thinks of risk as negative, as mitigating loss. I think of risk as a *positive opportunity*—a leveragable quantity to manage for financial gain. It's a big difference from the traditional thinking. And if we can show them we have the world's best data to back it up, they'll believe us."

Indeed it was a big difference. The idea that one company could actually "reposition" risk from negative to positive by disrupting the industry standard vision, backed by proprietary technology, led this multibillion-dollar insurance firm to a DSI for the first time in its history—not to mention the only DSI among all its competitors. They would be the first global firm to offer a proposition called *Return on Risk*.

When You're Done, Spread Your Candy on the Bed

In just a few days, you'll complete all your interviews. You'll have notes and quotes in what is potentially a very valuable $3.95 notebook. It's imperative to reread them right now and highlight key words, ideas, and starred passages with a marker. Or, if you're really gung ho and want to lock it all into your brain, type out all your notes. If you thought you'd glimpsed themes and threads of truth during your interviews, reviewing them all at once while they're still hot has a catalyzing effect. It launches you into the building phase of the DSI-making process where you'll be mixing your own common sense with the ideas and conclusions of others to determine the core of your real selling brand. It's your opportunity to challenge all the superficial conclusions you jumped to—that you promised yourself you wouldn't, but you did anyway—right from the first interview. Plus, by putting notes in the margins and colored dots or Post-it notes on key pages, you'll be indexing the important nuggets for later distillation into the DSI star itself.

Finishing Your R&D

Don't forget to include the "static" part of R&D at some point over the three-week period to round out your perspective. That is, read through the research reports, attitude-and-usage surveys, business plans, competitive focus group report summaries, and any other preexisting materials that the company has already spent thousands of dollars to acquire, and that will generally bear some additional fruit or help validate the interview fruit.

Finally, keep in mind that the R&D process is as much an art as a science and can be every bit as creative as any other part of the branding process. Bounce ideas around with others. Explore hunches. Ask a lot of "what ifs." You'll net better solutions.

Let's Summarize

You've just completed your R&D phase. Give yourself your first pat on the back because even if you quit right now, you're wiser about the current state of your brand and will make smarter communications decisions than you ever would without it. The entire process is cumulative that way, we promise. Here it is now, in brief:

Weeks 1–3

After you've reread the Granite Pages,

1. Choose twenty-five people to talk to—half inside, half outside if you can.
2. Make your list of ten to twelve questions, using the Eternal Questions as your guide.
3. Remind yourself of your objectives: you're listening for what's real versus what's imagined about:
   The current specialty,
   The key differentiators,
   The main weaknesses and inconsistencies in product and service,
   The competition, its strengths, and its weaknesses,
   What customers want most; what they're not getting now,
   The path to #1—the preemptable specialty that the company can become #1 in, leading to its DSI.
   You'll also be listening for and writing down all the nuggets of metaphor, language, and phrasing that can turn into points of the DSI star.
4. Schedule a one-to-three–day block to interview inside the company, catch as catch can on the Outside.
5. Create trust and rapport with the "container of trust." Use tactical listening skills.
6. Ask questions using the six honest serving men and question strings to narrow answers down to the level of truth.
7. Carefully review, annotate, or type out your notes to launch yourself into the creative phase of the process. Identify the persistent themes and expressions of pain, passion, and truth.
8. Review all preexisting research materials like competitive analyses, surveys, and research reports to validate or add to your learning.

9. Congratulate yourself on completing the most essential part of the process.

Time to hit the showers. Practice starts again at 8 A.M. on Monday.

CHAPTER 14

The Specialty You Will Own: Weeks 4 and 5

Now you're at the milestone where you'll ask the obligatory question, "Have I been granted the ingredients to make a soup or a salad? And if indeed salad, is it the Grilled Chicken Caesar or the House Tossed?"

Guru Mahatma Mahareshi "Mahesh" Goldberg

Two weeks from now, the raw material you've gathered from your R&D, mixed with your own instincts and experience, will be transformed into

1. The specialty you can be #1 in,
2. A definitive specialty statement,
3. Reduction of the above into your proposed DSI.

You'll have cracked the code for the DNA of your #1 brand because you'll have determined:

What attributes or performance specs do customers want most in your specialty, and where does the Sweet Spot lie between tangible promises and overpromises?

Which of the above are open to be claimed because a competitor does not already own them?

Which ones are possible for you to claim as is or turn into a new specialty because you have the capability and credibility to do it and be taken seriously?

Which ones can you afford to claim? When you add up the projected costs and logistics, which are you willing to invest the resources in to see all the way through to fulfillment of a #1 specialty?

The reason this simple, straightforward process is earmarked for two whole weeks is because of a general, creative rule called the Law of the Shower.

Law of the Shower

This is the rule that actually quantifies (1) the time-value of showers, (2) any drive longer than fifteen minutes, and (3) lying awake nights in the branding process. Sometimes the big answers pop up instantly during our endeavor. But others will require a modicum of time—time to mull, to daydream, to ponder, to question others you respect, and to weigh it all in your head. A cake needs a minimum time to bake and so do you.

While at DSI University, the Guru conducted a landmark study that showed the average mental gestation period for main elements of the DSI process—like choosing a name or a specialty—included approximately five hot showers, four drives, and three NSPs (nighttime sleepless periods).

So, what we'll be doing in this chapter is following a few orderly steps, sketching a simple chart or two to map our relative position versus competitors on paper, writing out our statements, and then applying the whole process to the Law of the Shower, until done.

Choosing a Specialty You Can Own—Quick Recap

After R&D, solving the question "What is the specialty we can be #1 in?" is the first step in the entire process, before we get to naming or any other element of the DSI star. Because as you'll recall, all buyers go through a mental process of elimination in which they first identify their own need, then match that to an industry/category, then to a specialty, and only then do they choose a brand which they consider #1 in that specialty. That brand "owns" the specialty.

When you examine your current specialty after your R&D and find that someone else already stands as #1 in it, you must declare #1 status in another unclaimed attribute or create a new specialty that's yours alone. That will become your Unique Ownable Specialty.

You can do that using any of the eight DSI templates. For example, Template 1, "The Preemptive Attribute DSI," adds a series of attribute "extenders" to your current "base specialty" until you separate yourself from the pack. If you wrote it out on the board, that process would look like this:

Base Specialty + *(Extender* + *Extender* + *Extender)* = Unique Ownable Specialty

Base Specialty	= Lager Beer
Extender 1	= German, Lager Beer
Extender 2	= Lite, German, Lager Beer
Extender 3	= Nonalcoholic, Lite, German, Lager Beer

= Unique Ownable Specialty

In the above case, it's arguable which of the extenders are simply attributes that keep you in the same specialty, and which are actually specialties themselves that shift you into a new base specialty. "Nonalcoholic" might easily be considered a whole new specialty in its own right, moving you all the way to a new base specialty as a result.

It's fun to debate, but there's no need to. The final destination—your Unique Ownable Specialty—is all we care about, regardless of the combination of gambits or templates we use to differentiate ourselves from the crowd.

The Big Question: To Switch or Not to Switch Specialties

It's clear by now that if there are eight competitors in your current specialty and none of them stand for anything superlative, you certainly don't need to invent yourself into a whole new specialty or category. Just find out what your customers think is the most important key attribute in your specialty when they make buying decisions, then claim it loudly, proudly, and memorably as your own. Your competitors will be the ones who need to claim the lesser attributes or invent new specialties if they want to gain market share.

But maybe you do need to vault into a new specialty because all the important attributes are taken. Either way, you've got to take the first step to making this decision right now—by mining the answers you have in your R&D interview notes to questions like:

What would you call your base specialty—what do you do best or do that nobody else does? Who are your competitors? What are they famous for? Who's #1 in the specialty? What makes them #1? Do customers consider them #1? What's most important to customers when they buy? And then plotting yourself versus your competitors on a virtual grid we call the specialty map, which will show you where you can go from here.

Okay, Let's Get Started

"What's Our Present Specialty?" Don't Skip This . . .
We'll start here because, as obvious as you might think it is ("What, you don't think I know what business I'm in? There's a sign on the building. It says FUNERAL PARLOR, for @#%% sakes."), we're amazed at how many times we ask this in meetings with senior management and the debate gets so heated, we have to postpone the rest of the agenda.

Even if you think you're absolutely positive of where you

are at the start of this process, do what aircraft pilots call a quick scan to double-check one last time before changing to a new heading. Take the learning from your recent interviews and ask the question anew.

Here's why: Let's say you own a chain of high-end camera stores. Along with the digital photo revolution, you've branched into video equipment with all the peripherals. You've got a catalog and an eCommerce Web site for wholesale customers, which, combined, bring in as much business as your walk-in stores. You used to sell just to professionals, but now the serious amateurs are generating big revenue.

You've always assumed you're simply a camera shop. But maybe reality has shifted. You may have evolved into an imaging specialist, an exclusive professional retail store, or a direct channel reseller. Again, this isn't yet about what specialty you might want to move to. It's about finding the true longitude and latitude of where you are now before moving forward. Based on the business you're conducting today, what is your specialty? The answer isn't creative—it's empirical. Discuss it with your colleagues, check your notes if necessary, make the call, and put it on paper. Then you can plot the red "we're here" dot on the specialty map.

The Specialty Map

Once you plot your standing in key attributes, you can decide to stay in your specialty or move onward because you'll see if you're blocked from #1 by someone above you. If so, you'll see where the best openings are.

Construct the map as follows:

First, make a list of the generally accepted key attributes in your base specialty. If it were fiberglass cruising sailboats, you might have:

Speed
Sea worthiness
Construction quality

Class popularity
Roominess below
Economy
High technology
. . . and so on.

Next, from your interview notes, take the up-to-date list of (1) your current competitors, (2) the key attributes in your specialty that are most important to buyers (don't forget to gauge for the Sweet Spot), and (3) the rankings that customers and outside stakeholders would knowingly give to each competitor for each attribute. Include yourself. Then make the following table on a pad of paper or a spread sheet.

On the left, next to the vertical margin, list your competitors. Along the horizontal margin, list the motivating attributes for customers in order from most important to least important, left to right. Then, mark either a "1" for the #1 rank or a "2" on the grid for each company that ranks as 1 or 2 in a particular attribute. Leave all others blank. The public has to perceive this ranking or the company gets a blank.

Specialty Attributes in the Sweet Spot

	A1	A2	A3	A4	A5	A6	A7	A8	A9
Company A	1	2							
Company B		1							
Company C						1		2	
Company D			1					1	
Company E			2				2		
Us							1		

The reason we only rank 1 and 2 is that there's normally room for a clear first and second like Coke and Pepsi or Hertz and Avis in any specialty. Sometimes they engage in a horse race, jockeying back and forth.

Beyond that, for practical purposes, the next rank is 3 to infinity and is useless in this exercise. Because not only is it seldom possible to rank the rest of the field accurately beyond number 2, it's irrelevant. If there's a credible #1 already in place above us, not to mention a credible 2, we're not going to preempt that column. We've got to choose another attribute to be the best in within our specialty—or make the decision to extend ourselves into a new specialty with its own set of key attributes.

Reading the Map

Like everything else in real branding, the answers you divine from the specialty map have much more to do with common sense than brain surgery, so they sometimes seem pedestrian in hindsight. But fundamentals always do. What's important is that you think in steps that resemble the specialty map grid, even if you don't actually write it down.

But trust us—it can be amazingly clarifying and centering to see on paper in the light of day that a competitor owns a lock on "speed" and another owns "old-fashioned, Maine construction quality." They won't be displaced in your lifetime, even though your boats, too, are fast and well built. Too bad.

But "roomy below," which means comfortable, and "high tech," which means easy and safe above-deck for weekenders to sail, are in growing demand and wide open for the taking. A real brand can easily be hung on the "#1 boats for easy cruising comfort—because they have the best combination of high tech controls above with feng shui below." It's a Unique Ownable Specialty.

Speciality Attributes in the Sweet Spot

	Speed	Sea Worthiness	Construction Quality	Class Popularity	Room Below	Economy	High Tech
Kingman Yachts	1	2					
Parker Boats						2	
Offshore Corp.		1	1				
Cape Craft				2		1	
Northeast Yacht			2				
Gulf Marine	2			1			
Us							

And if all the attributes are taken, consider a literal split into a new base specialty. If all your competitors are in traditional single hulls (as they were not too long ago), design yourself a two-hulled catamaran and start with a clean specialty slate: "comfortable, high tech catamarans."

Picking the Winner for Your DSI

Often times you'll look at the specialty map, make realistic assessments, and realize there are more than one—maybe three or more—potential #1 specialties that could make your mouth water. Johnny would grab greedily at them all. You've got to commit and coolly pick the winner.

Once again, all you need is a white board with a fresh set of markers or a pad of paper to conduct the following, fundamental scoring test:

Ten Criteria for the Winning Specialty

Criteria	Rating 1–5 (Best)

1. Superlative:　　　　　　　　　　1 2 3 4 5
Can you perform this function as well or better
than any one else? Is it something you can do
best?

2. Simple, Understandable, and Relatable:　1 2 3 4 5
Is it quickly obvious as a superior proposition
with key benefit associations? Is it too high
level to identify with, or is it in the Sweet Spot?

3. Preawareness Level:　　　　　　　　1 2 3 4 5
Does it point to a solution the target already
knows it needs? If education is required, is the
point simply grasped?

4. Importance:　　　　　　　　　　　1 2 3 4 5
Does it address a top issue for decision makers?

5. Believable:　　　　　　　　　　　1 2 3 4 5
Is it credible for us to say? Do we have a
logical "reason why"? Will the market perceive
it is within our domain? Does it connect with
our prior competency?

6. Measurable:　　　　　　　　　　　1 2 3 4 5
Does it lend itself to objective measurement
not only by customers but by us so we can
gauge progress and improvements?

7. Ownable:　　　　　　　　　　　　1 2 3 4 5
Is it a proprietary, or is it available to be
exclusively ours?

8. Protectable:　　　　　　　　　　　1 2 3 4 5
Are there barriers to entry or can we
erect them?

9. Feasible and Affordable: 1 2 3 4 5
Is it feasible to make real and tangible by our
actions in a realistic time frame? Do we have
the technology and expertise, or can we afford
the investment to get it and deliver what we
promise?

10. Marchable to: 1 2 3 4 5
When all is said and done, will our people
march to it, rally around it, embrace it, and
accept it as a legitimate compass to guide the
business at large?

Now add up the scores and hope that the winner was the
one you liked best to begin with. If there's no obvious winner
or if the scorers can't agree, you should test. What we recommend is that you write out a specialty statement for each one
using the simple format set forth below and test those. We'll
talk about testing at the end of the chapter. In any case,
whether you decide to test or not, this is your next step: writing your specialty statement.

Writing Your Specialty Statement

Some people refer to this as a "statement of positioning." We
call it the specialty statement because ours is a sharper requirement—a position that's #1 in a specialty by definition. In
any case, your specialty statement is the first and most important set of words you're going to create during the entire
process of establishing your real selling brand. It's the internal
stake in the ground that doubles as a lightning rod for all else
that follows.

It's not meant to be your tag line, although nothing says that
something close to it can't eventually be. It's a two-sentence
declaration of the specialty you are #1 in plus the key "reason
why," meaning it's where you drop the gauntlet and declare,
"*This*, attached to our name, is what our proposed DSI will be."

It's more important that the language of the specialty statement be dead-on accurate than sound pretty, clever, or metaphorical. That comes later in all the external expression of the DSI star and beyond. The first job responsibility of this statement is internal—it's literally the needle of your compass. It's like legal language in that sense. It's meant to align and point your business. If it's heard or seen by the outside world, no problem. But external consumption is not primarily what it's here for. The specialty statement is the place to state it exactly right, not state it remarkably.

Simple Specialty Statement Structure

Here's a sample:

_____ (Product/Company) is the #1 choice for _____ (Specialty). That's because only _____ (Product/Company) has _____ (A Unique Reason Why: a superlative ingredient, process, or service that others don't).

As you can see, the hard part isn't writing it; it's all the courageous, objective mature choosing you did beforehand to commit to the specialty you'll own.

If you've done that, you don't need creative copywriters or agency people to write this down. You'll do it best. Just keep scribbling variations until you can feel you've got the crispest, most exacting essence that you can put into two sentences.

Also keep in mind that the specialty can be either "an atom or a molecule"—that is, one element or a unique combination of elements, whatever the base specialty plus extenders are that describe you (neonatal pediatric cardiology, for example). Similarly, your Unique Reason Why is either a single element or a unique combination that others don't or can't claim the way you do.

Going back to your fiberglass cruising sailboat company, your specialty statement would become:

XYZ Yachts are the #1 choice in high comfort, high tech sailboats because they're the only ones designed by naval architects who are also certified in feng shui.

Here're some more:

eHarmony.com is the #1 choice for dating services that get me married. That's because it's the only one with a test for twenty-nine areas of compatibility.

WeatherBug is the #1 choice for accurate, localized weather reports. That's because it's the only one with a reporting station in every neighborhood, not just the airport.

Hefty Bags are the #1 choice for tough, unbreakable trash bags. That's because they're the only ones made with triple-polymer plastics.

Budweiser is the #1 choice for American lager beer. That's because it's the only one specifically brewed for working men like me.

Nike is the #1 choice for elite athletic shoes. That's because they're the ones that more sports heroes wear.

Dr. Joseph Della Russo is the #1 choice for fail-safe "lasik" eye surgery. That's because he does twice as many surgeries as any other doctor in the tri-state area.

ProFlowers.com is the #1 choice for sending the freshest, lowest-priced flowers. That's because

they're the only ones that are shipped <u>directly</u>
<u>from the flower fields to you.</u>

<u>*Hooters*</u> *is the #1 choice in casual, fried-food and*
<u>drink chains for guys</u>. That's because they're the
one that <u>guarantees the Hooters</u>.

<u>*AFLAC*</u> *is the #1 choice for <u>uhhhh . . . mmm . . .</u>*
<u>errr . . . I know this . . . hang on . . . I'll get it.</u>
They're the one with a <u>comedy duck</u>.

We apologize in advance to all those who are going to sue us, but we just can't help it with the duck.

Anyhow, you can see how those simple little specialty statements are put together. We're not holding you to these specific format words every time. Whether you write, "We're the company that," or "the best company," or "the #1 choice," it's the superlative expression that matters. And it doesn't matter if there's an extra tier or two in your "reason why" either. Use an extra "that means" or a double "because" if you need it for clarity. The elements are what matter. "We're #1 in this important specialty because we do something credible that no one else does." "We're best at this, because we do that."

Finally, remember that the specialty statement is technically not the DSI itself, even though it's getting awfully damn close. The Dominant Selling Idea is a verbal or visual snapshot of the #1 specialty attached to your name in the customer's mind. In other words, we doubt that any customer consciously verbalizes the specific words of the specialty statements above. In their brains, they might get a flash of "safest car." The specialty statement is the structural frame we use to guide our messaging in the hopes of yielding that flash of thought. A whole automobile company has to rally to the statement, "Volvo: the #1 choice in safe, moderate-status, European cars. That's because it's the only one designed for safety from the inside out," so that a customer will later think to herself, Volvo = Safety.

Losing That Last Five Pounds: Checking for Your Dominant Selling Idea

With your one specialty statement or top finalists in hand, you've come a long way, baby. Now it's worth subjecting what you've got to one more filter—projecting it forward to see how it ultimately will play as a real Dominant Selling Idea. That is, will it reduce down to a one- or two-word snapshot that you might effectively "own" in your customers' heads. We must constantly remind ourselves that the customers' mind is the only prize we're after and that our ultimate Dominant Selling Idea will result from the net fusion of all the points of the DSI star, plus all our communications, our performance at every touch point, etc.

Recapping our earliest DSI discussion, we want to trigger an elementary thought in the customers' mind like . . .

"*I know XYZ. They're:*

The only one with _____. *The only one with a Tootsie Roll center.*

The best _____. *The best TV picture.*

The #1 _____. *The #1 car rental company.*

The most famous _____ for _____. *The most famous island for scuba.*

The _____ est _____. *The fastest car.*

The _____ company. *The Consumer Driven Health Insurance Company.*

The _____ that _____. *The soup that comes with great big chunks.*"

Another way to look at this is to recognize that each of the above brands purports to own something in their category or specialty: Tootsie Roll center (in lollipops), picture (in TVs), popularity (in car rental), scuba (in the Islands), speed (in cars), the consumer (in health care), heartiness (in soup).

What do the specialty statements we listed earlier say that they own?

eHarmony.com . . . marriage
WeatherBug . . . accuracy
Hefty Bags . . . toughness
Budweiser . . . working man
Nike . . . favorite athletes
Dr. Joseph Della Russo . . . experience
ProFlowers.com . . . fresh/price combo
Hooters . . . Hooters
AFLAC . . .

Do this check and make sure the specialty statement points to the word or snippet you want to own. That's where all this is going. If it's unclear, or if it's somehow not just the right word, it's worth adjusting until you're sure it's dead on the mark.

Testing

There are often times when the process yields one and only one specialty statement that's so patently obvious, there's really no second. Congrats. You've saved yourself a week. But when you go through the Ten Criteria exercise plus your gut check and you get down to two or three finalists but no clear winner, there's no excuse for and no equity in not testing.

Professional qualitative and quantitative market research that measures attitudes, motivation, and consumer reasoning is an entire field unto itself, which is well beyond our scope here. You can spend hundreds of thousands on it and months doing it.

But that's not what we're suggesting at this juncture. By testing, we're talking about an exercise that's empirical, factual, and simple—what the original mail order marketers used to call "copy testing." It seeks not to understand, it seeks to score what works versus what doesn't work, period. The understanding comes in hindsight.

And we're talking about having the will—an attitude really—where you're willing to submit your ideas to outside parties, force yourself not to bias the answers, and actually hear subjective reactions that may be entirely different than your own. In other words, being able to admit that your favorite out of five choices—even if you're the CEO—may be the least popular or correct choice.

Last, the process does not have to be lengthy, tedious, or complex at all to be effective. In other words, you can do it yourself in the most rudimentary, straightforward of ways and get the direction you're after.

The main thing (as in so much of what we've talked about in this book) is that you do anything at all because so many companies do virtually nothing in this regard.

Devising Your Own Simple Tests

The key to success is to keep it uncomplicated and unbiased and to use the least number of variables. You want one-to-one exchanges versus groups because groups poison themselves with shared opinions. And you want to simulate uninfluenced consumer choice wherever possible.

For example, if you had three book titles you wanted to test to see which had the most counter appeal, the simplest idea would be to put them on a counter, in effect, and watch what consumers do. Print out three identical-looking covers, the only difference being the title. Put all three in front of your target group. Explain nothing. Just say, "Here are three free books. You can only pick one. Which do you pick?" Then keep an honest tally.

"Putting the test in front of targets" can mean almost any scenario you can come up with. You can go to the food court at the mall yourself, stop people briefly, and ask for their choice. They'll give it to you. You can hire professionals at a test facility to do it. You can go to your local book store if you know the owner. E-mail a PDF file to your business Rolodex. Or show it to friends and even family and get completely legitimate data—so long as you do not cheat and hint at the winner you're after.

Bottom line, the only meaningful tests are the ones where you enable respondents to choose between equals, no questions asked—allowing them to assign all the value differential.

This is how you test specialty statements. Print up to five choices and ask targets to pick. This is how you test DSI phrases. This is how you test names and tag lines.

Only after they've chosen, ask them to tell you why in a sentence or two and take notes, which will deepen your understanding.

Getting Professional Help in Testing

If time, budget, or inclination permits, there's no reason not to contact a professional research person or firm to broaden your perspective.

To choose a research group, remember two things:

1. Big, expensive firm does not necessarily mean better. Many of the very best people are former top research executives who have started their own independent firms. The quality of the person on your business is all that counts.
2. Have confidence in your own BS meter when judging research proposals. When the researcher can't make you understand her methods in practical terms because the process is too special and proprietary, or if it sounds too far out and theoretical—it probably is.

Conclusion: The Commonsense Testing Rules of Thumb

1. In testing, less is not more. A sample of thirty is better than a sample of five. Two venues are better than one, etc.
2. You can accomplish a lot in a short time for very little money. If you and your test are objective, you can learn a significant amount in one or two days. If you have the time and budget, set up tests in multiple geographies to account for regional factors. It's your judgment. See number 1 above.
3. Doing *anything* is a quantum step better than doing nothing.
4. Try to test only one variable at time, keeping all else—words, phrasing colors, graphics—as equal as possible so you can tell exactly where the delta resides.

For example, if you're testing for the most powerful "that's because/reason why" phrase in your specialty statement, then try to use the exact same declaration sentence in each case—for example,

   a. WeatherBug is the #1 choice for accurate, localized weather. *That's because it has ten times more weather stations than anyone else.*
   b. WeatherBug is the #1 choice for accurate, localized weather. *That's because it's the only one with technology that reports every second, not every hour.*
   c. WeatherBug is the #1 choice for accurate, localized weather. *That's because it's the only one with weather stations right in your neighborhood—not just out at the airport.*

Ultimately, it's more important to have common sense and objectivity in conducting empirical tests than a Ph.D. And as in all things marketing, even empirical results are always subject to the gut test at the end. You seldom get such a clear mandate in anything that it's a thirty-to-one slam dunk. When the results are reasonably close and you've at least done your "disaster check," you needn't be afraid to pick the one that didn't win numerically if your instinct tells you. It has to feel right. It has to motivate you and your colleagues because it's going to be the rallying cry you go to battle with.

CHAPTER 15

The Brand Story: Week 6

You can make a speech with wonderful facts, figures and data. Ten minutes later, a person will have forgotten 99 percent. But tell a man a story, and twenty years later he can come back to you and recount every word you said.

Guru Mahatma Mahareshi "Mahesh" Goldberg

All great communicators tell stories. Great salespeople, great teachers, great speech makers, and great leaders all routinely tap into this universal connective mechanism. Ronald Reagan, nicknamed the Great Communicator, didn't start an important policy speech with oratorical prose, facts, and figures. He'd tell you a story about a little girl in a yellow dress, living in Communist Poland. Within minutes, he had the crowd mesmerized.

The hypnotic power of story draws people into a world of emotion, color, and familiar experience of their own making, creating irresistible identifications. And the inherent associative structure of a well-crafted story makes it the most efficient way to package long strings of information for indelible input into the memory.

In short, people not only love stories, they literally crave stories—like a basic mental foodstuff for proper psychic nourishment. Just look at the billions of dollars worth of stories that are consumed worldwide every day in the form of movies, television, magazines, books, and other entertainment. It's obviously more than a luxury. It's a need.

Why are we going on about this?

Because every brand is like a story too. It's the story of what you stand for, why you stand for it, how you got to the point where you stand for it better than anyone else, and where it's going to lead you. It can be explained with a beginning, a middle, and an end, starting with "There was this problem. Then a company decided to help people with this problem by creating a new and better solution. The solution helped people not only in one big way, but lots of little ways as well. Now the world is a better, happier place. Maybe we can help you."

In short, to communicate as effectively as we can, anything that *can* be packaged into story form *should* be packaged into story form. Brands are no exception.

So at this point, we'll take the "what, how, and why" of our Unique Ownable Specialty and write it down in a one- to two-page narrative, the *brand story*.

A Living Document

The brand story will be like the "executive summary" for your brand. As it evolves over time, it should house the key selling language, Golden Metaphors, and special phrasing you gain from your continuing consumer dialogue and experience in the field. We call these *key language threads*, which you'll want to utilize as much as possible in all communications. You'll always gather new data and get smarter the longer you live with your brand. As you develop your naming structure, DSI tag lines, DSI performance examples, and more, you'll want to build those in as well.

So consider the brand story to be a living document. Add to it, improve it, and constantly check it for freshness as you continue on your path. It will be the domicile of your core brand message, a guideline for communications in any medium from PR to TV to sales presentations to your "elevator pitch."

Writing Your Own Brand Story

The following are four real company brand stories. By reading them, you'll see that the prompt for writing your own is really straightforward. In fact, you got assignments just like this in seventh grade. You handed it in and got a B+, just like we did:

1. Write it like a story narrative—one to three pages long.
2. It's about your Unique Ownable Specialty.
3. Describe the problem and who it affected. What was the need?
4. Introduce the solution—what you saw and did to solve it.
5. Explain how and why it works that should make it believable.
6. Describe the customers' experience now.
7. Describe the continuing promise.
8. Salt it with the language, expressions, and key message threads you've gleaned from your R&D interview process and your focused brand thinking from the past several weeks.
9. Avoid too much jargon—but it's OK to use industry-accepted terms and professional phrasing that not all "civilians" will get. Sometimes that makes it more familiar and credible to your target readers.

Here are real life examples to get you started.

Brand Story 1: A global insurance broker and risk management firm

SPECIALTY STATEMENT: Aon Healthcare is the #1 choice for corporations who want maximum ROR™ (Return on Risk™). That's because Aon has created the industry's most advanced data center and data-based tools to quantify solutions for the first time.

DSI TEMPLATE: The template used here is a combination of "the transplant" with a "magic-ingredient" reason why. The company took the venerable business term *return on investment (ROI)* and transplanted *risk* to create a new specialty called *Return on Risk (ROR)*. The magic-ingredient reason why is that ROR solutions are powered by the Center for Predictive Data—the most advanced data resource center in the industry.

BRAND STORY

Forward-thinking risk managers, CFOs, CEOs, consultants, and analysts agree: the business of risk management has changed radically in the past few years. The days when all a client had to do was call a broker and buy an insurance policy for a competitive price are over. Today, they're navigating on a sea of risk where all aspects of the organization—finance, operations, human capital, and product performance—either impact, or are impacted by, risk. The financial health and overall competitiveness of the organization are increasingly affected by the course that's taken.

Over the past decade, a concept called Enterprise Risk Management (ERM) has been advanced as a more holistic approach to risk. But for many, ERM is a great idea that has not been fulfilled, either because it was too ambitious in scope to be practically applied, because the critical supportive data wasn't available, or because ERM focused too much on identifying problems—not on the tools to solve those problems or measure the improvements. The risk arena needed something more.

Now Aon Healthcare is announcing the next generation of risk management solutions that will meet these needs—a system that combines:

- The global approach to risk pioneered by ERM,
- The advanced data tools necessary to make this approach a reality,

- Modular, incremental scope to benefit any size institution
- Seamless integration of Aon's nationwide professional resources, and, above all,
- A total-results focus that finally connects all the dots from problem to solution to bottom line.

Aon calls it ROR™: the solutions that maximize Return on Risk.

ROR solutions shift the entire framework of risk management from negative to positive. ROR leverages the new complexities, transforming risk into an area of opportunity and competitive advantage for those who embrace it with the right attitude, data, tools, and resources. Now the goal for every organization can and should be to optimize Return on Risk for maximum financial and competitive advantage.

Unlike earlier programs in ERM, the ROR process can be delivered in a modular, incremental approach, recognizing that every positive step that lowers costs and reduces claims contributes to the bottom line. But ROR does more. By measuring the key drivers of risk within an organization, then delivering on the promise with a proprietary set of tools, organizations will see exponential improvement. For example, a hospital that measures and improves its medical outcomes not only will see reductions in medical liability costs, but will also improve nurse retention, improve patient safety and satisfaction, lower workers' compensation costs, and strengthen its brand in the community. A financial institution that reduces its operational risk not only improves its professional liability costs, it also reduces its liquidity requirements and improves its profitability.

ROR is a visionary approach, a proprietary process that tailors itself to the client's organization, and a practical set of tools that utilize advanced data for measurable improvements and bottom-line results.

THE CENTER FOR PREDICTIVE DATA Aon recognizes that ground-breaking approaches like ROR require ground-breaking tools and resources in order to succeed. No factor is more essential to ROR than the ready availability of advanced, accurate, and affordable data—packaged into both off-the-shelf and custom tools. Simply put: data is the backbone of ROR solutions. As the first in a series of permanent initiatives, we formed the Aon Center for Predictive Data (CPD)—an entity whose mission is to collect, integrate, research, improve, and otherwise advance the science of data utilization for professionals whose goal is to generate a Return on Risk. The CPD is a premier information clearinghouse for clients, industry and government officials, offering both public and private data resources for organizational benchmarking, cost analysis, and operations improvement.

With its combination of data resources, professional resources, global approach, and flexible applications, Aon is proud to lead risk management into the era of "Return on Risk" management—guiding our clients to lower costs, greater profits, better patient outcomes, and competitive advantage in the new millenium.

Brand Story 2: A national back-office services company specializing in private charitable foundations

SPECIALTY STATEMENT: Foundation Source is the #1 choice for complete outsourced support services for private foundations. That's because Foundation Source has the first and only technology that automates and streamlines the foundation administrative process.

DSI TEMPLATE: It's the "pure original." No company has ever successfully automated the administrative process for private charitable foundations, until now.

BRAND STORY

For over one hundred years, private charitable foundations have been the giving vehicle of choice for America's prominent families because of the tax benefits, financial flexibility, and legacy benefits they provide.

But through the years, as new rules and regulations made governance more complex and time consuming, foundation administration remained a traditional, paper-based process—not keeping up with the cost- and time-saving efficiencies enjoyed by other modern industries.

The result for too many directors and staff is that running a foundation has become a technical, clerical, and compliance burden that prevents them from spending enough time in the charitable community—the real work of philanthropy. Their overall sense of satisfaction is reduced and the impact their foundations have is diminished as well.

Foundation Source has brought a fundamental change to the world of foundation-based philanthropy that traditionally run foundations can't provide. A Foundation Source foundation is stronger, is more audit-proof, and provides maximum impact in its community. Our combination of back-office systems, convenient online services, and "on-call" experts provides a more satisfying, effective, and supportive experience for donors, family members, directors, and staff. For new foundations, our modern systems remove the barriers of high start-up expense and complex maintenance which kept foundations the exclusive vehicle of the superwealthy.

Foundation Source pioneered and perfected the use of computer and online technology to automate the most burdensome administrative, compliance, tax-filing, and grant-management details for the properly run foundation. We've made the most labor-intensive duties of the back office more manageable while providing convenient, centralized monitoring tools for everyone involved.

For directors and professional administrators, Foundation

Source works as the "staff's staff"—taking care of sophisticated monitoring and record keeping behind the scenes while taking on whatever administrative chores the staff chooses for us to handle, allowing them to focus on their most important and effective tasks.

For attorneys and other advisers, Foundation Source is both a risk manager and an online monitoring resource, enabling them to oversee compliance instantly from any computer desktop and to be assured that all data is automatically tracked and centrally stored for immediate retrieval.

For donors and their families, Foundation Source means not just a better foundation but "a better foundation experience" in every aspect. Now they can focus on the needs of the community, grant making, family collaboration, the philanthropic mission, or any other priorities they prefer.

For all of these reasons, Foundation Source has become the #1 provider of support services in the areas of administration, compliance monitoring, tax filing, and grant management. And that's why our clients trust us as *the Silent Partner behind America's Foundations*, allowing them to fulfill their philanthropic mission without conflict or compromise.

Brand Story 3: **A company that manufactures computerized "personal trainers" that are attached to fitness club equipment.**
SPECIALTY STATEMENT: FitLinxx is the #1 choice in computer-assisted fitness training. That's because it's the only equipment with Fitness Intelligence Technology™.

DSI TEMPLATE: Both the promise and reasons why are "pure originals."

BRAND STORY:
THE THIRD REVOLUTION IN FITNESS—FITNESS INTELLIGENCE FOR THE AVERAGE EXERCISER. There have been two revolutions

in the science of fitness in the past fifty years. The first established proper *methods* of exercise—"guided form" using machines—and standards for intensity and duration. The second, more recent revolution introduced the *psychology* of exercise, with the realization that motivation of the mind is just as important as proper method for the body in achieving results. Unfortunately, these advances have not reached as many people as they should have. Without ongoing coaching, most average exercisers continue to use poor form and lack motivational tools, leading to poor results and poor commitment.

Now, a company called FitLinxx has overcome this problem, creating the third revolution—the *fitness intelligence* revolution. What FitLinxx has done, for the first time, is to add intelligent technology directly to a full range of strength and cardiovascular fitness equipment; then network them together to link proper, consistent exercise motion with enhanced motivation for everyone. The result is truly ground-breaking: a faster, easier, safer, more motivating fitness experience for the millions of exercisers who are turning to fitness centers for a more balanced, healthy lifestyle.

FitLinxx's fitness intelligence technology (FIT) enables every machine to effectively "learn" each individual's personalized program, "coach" for proper settings and correct form, and "track" exact workout progress, exercise by exercise, over the in-facility network, as well as out onto the Internet. This gives members the edge in achieving their goals. It gives fitness centers the edge in tracking, supporting, and retaining current members, and the edge in attracting new ones.

FitLinxx provides the "missing link" for the balanced lifestyle seekers—the major growth segment who now make up over 60 percent of the fitness market. By linking a more positive mental experience to a more productive physical one in every exercise and every workout, it produces less stress, more success. It's called "the intelligent workout."

THE INTELLIGENT WORKOUT: GOOD FOR MEMBERS, STAFF, AND FITNESS CENTERS. By adding fitness intelligence technology directly to the existing strength and cardio machines in the fitness center and then networking them together, benefits that were impossible in the old world of paper workouts and stand-alone preintelligent machines are now possible for everyone—benefits like:

1. A more powerful mind-and-body connection for members. The handholding and feedback from FitLinxx makes exercisers more confident, enthusiastic, and motivated right from their first workout. And the interactive "coaching" gets members using proper form in every session, which in turn leads to better physical results. Combining improved mental motivation and proper exercise form gives the balanced lifestyle seekers a much higher prospect of locking in the new lifestyle they seek and staying with their fitness program long-term.

2. Enhanced instructor/member relationships through better information. Fitness instructors are more effective and professional, because they have access to practical, simple-to-use information about all their members' progress. Because all FitLinxx data is networked back to a central staff monitoring station, instructors are able to easily identify members at key moments of need, and help a larger number of members succeed. It also allows managers to measure instructors' performance and hold them accountable for results.

3. Increased rates of new-member sales and current-member retention for fitness centers. Prospective members instantly see greater "fitness floor appeal"—a cutting-edge, high-visibility differentiator—when they tour a FitLinxx-powered facility. This leads to greater attraction, better "word of mouth," and higher close rates, especially in more competitive markets. What's more, FitLinxx's unique ability to link motivation and form for better member results leads to a 54 percent higher retention rate.

THE PIONEER AND WORLD LEADER Fitness intelligence technology is rapidly becoming an established category, essential to the operations of fitness centers worldwide. As the world market for FIT continues to grow rapidly, FitLinxx has emerged as the clear leader in features, functions, ease of use, installations, and industry support. *FitLinxx: The Edge Is the Intelligence.*

Brand Story 4: A company that provides systems and training for 911 emergency dispatchers

SPECIALTY STATEMENT: Total Response is the #1 choice for Computer Aided Call Handling (CACH), the next generation of call handling™ that can integrate police, fire, and medical in a single call. That's because Total Response invented and perfected CACH technology, giving it the most expertise.

DSI TEMPLATE: "The Transplant": Total Response transplanted a call-handling system into computer-aided dispatch (CAD) technology for the first time, creating the new specialty called CACH.

BRAND STORY

EMERGENCY DISPATCH TODAY—DOING MORE WITH LESS. In all areas of emergency dispatch, professionals are being asked to do more with less. The incident numbers are increasing and call volumes are skyrocketing. Cell phones make multiple-party 911 calls the norm. Small local emergencies can turn into homeland threats. The public wants higher and higher levels of customer service, the legal community threatens greater liability, and political powers demand constant accountability. Call handlers must be ready to act as the first lifeline to victims and first intelligence for responders. Call dispatchers must provide the correct response. Both have to know more and do more every day, just to keep up. Add the pressure of staff and resource freezes and cutbacks, and it's inevitable that stress levels and turnover are increasing as well.

FIRST BREAKTHROUGH, NOT ENOUGH. The first breakthrough in emergency dispatch was Computer-aided dispatch. CAD applied the power of computers to the "back end" of the dispatch process—organizing, tracking, and dispatching assets for the most efficient, intelligent response. Introduced over a decade ago, CAD has become the standard for departments across the country. The problem was that the "front end"—initial call handling—was not up to speed. Manual systems and paper-and-pencil management were keeping CAD from reaching its potential.

CACH: THE NEXT GENERATION OF CALL HANDLING, HERE NOW. Now the "front end" of the equation, call handling, has achieved a similar breakthrough—the power of true computer integration and automation at the fingertips of every call taker. A system that finally makes emergency dispatch a completely computer-aided process from the first call for help, straight through to the arrival of the right responders with the right information at the right time.

It's called Computer Aided Call Handling ™ (CACH), and only Total Response has it. It's the technology that makes your system an "end-to-end" computer-aided system for the first time.

CACH is far more than a card-based manual placed onto a computer screen. CACH has been designed from software engine through user navigation to maximize ease of use with the full power, speed, and integration of features that modern computing commands. To create CACH, we took the world's most reliable, fault-tolerant computer technology and combined it with the world's most experienced and widely used emergency communications training protocols to create a best-of-breed system that revolutionizes call handling on all levels. CACH means:

1. The first true, seamless integration of the three service areas (police, fire, and medical) into one fast, dynamic emer-

gency protocol. It eliminates the separation or disconnect between call handler and caller when seconds save lives.

2. More rapid, integrated prioritization. It avoids dangerous conflicts and misinterpretation of priorities when multiple call handlers must participate on calls.

3. Perspective to "triangulate" the appropriate response instantly among the three service areas.

4. A user-tested, simple, and intuitive user interface that requires minimal training.

5. Power to "scale on the fly" to any level—from the smallest local incident to large-scale emergencies and homeland threats.

6. "Guided flexibility" of protocols to empower the professional with tools for any situation, no matter how unusual, while still providing clear limits and guidelines.

7. The world's most proven emergency telecommunications experience and training at the side of every call taker on every call—like a partner—making call handling a consistent process at every console on every shift.

Whether you're a major metropolitan call center or single-unit municipal PSAP, CACH from Total Response is the missing piece that emergency dispatch—and CAD systems above all—have been waiting for. This new integrated solution for a new generation of PSD is called CACH/CAD. It's an idea that will save time, stress, assets, and, most of all, lives.

Brand Story as Elevator Pitch

Q: *What exactly do you say to the CEO of your top sales prospect when you find yourself alone with him on the express elevator from the forty-fourth floor and you've got about one minute to make him understand your value proposition, get interested, and agree to make an appointment with you on Monday?*

A: It's all right there in your brand story. While almost nobody agrees on exactly what an "elevator pitch" is, we'd say the best definition is the following: An elevator pitch is your brand story shortened by about two thirds; to about a half a page or 120 words—the amount you can comfortably speak in about a minute. Since you don't have time or permission to set up the linear problem–solution structure of your full manifesto, you invert your brand story structure to capture interest and attention first, then explain the details. That means you open with your solution first—your stunning promise of value—then recap with details of the problem solved, the insights that led to your solution, and the unique "reasons why" it's all credible.

Writing an elevator pitch isn't a mandatory step toward building the five-point star of your DSI—it's more of a sales tool. But it's great practice and a great discipline, a bonus that you'll relish having in your pocket whenever the moment arises—one that every single employee should be able to relate instantly to anyone on the outside. We highly recommend taking an hour to write one.

My, how the time flies! Just like that, you're about to become seniors at DSI University, ready to go forth and change the world! It seems like only yesterday you were arriving, starry-eyed freshmen, wet behind the ears.

Actually, if you're a fast reader, it probably *was* only yesterday. Well just 'cause this was quick, don't think we won't be hitting you up for cash for the new hockey rink the second you're out of here, either. We've got to keep up with Harvard.

So lets begin our home stretch, weeks seven and eight—where we will walk our new brand into the promised land.

CHAPTER 16

Turning on the Juice:
Weeks 7 and 8

"The time has come," the Walrus said, "To talk of many things: Of shoes—and ships—and sealing-wax, Of cabbages, and kings; And why the sea is boiling hot and there's soy bean buffalo wings—And a bleach breakthrough, called Protein II, that cleans your bathtub ring."

Guru Mahatma Mahareshi "Mahesh" Goldberg

If the proposed DSI we've just created is our electrical power source, then naming, DSI tag lines, key visual, and DSI-level performance are the halogen bulbs that are going to illuminate the DSI star and send its rays into the minds of our customers.

We can do a lot in the next two weeks, even light a point or two of the star in that time. For example, it's not uncommon for a great new name to have already reared its lovely head sometime in the past six weeks, between all your interviews, your discussions, and your ruminations in the shower. Likewise for a DSI tag and some inspired performance-aligning ideas. Or, you might be right on the cusp and nail it down in weeks seven and eight by conducting a focused naming or tag line exercise, what those in the business call an "exploratory."

But don't expect to finish.

Not that you absolutely can't, but you don't need to and shouldn't force yourself to, any more than you can ask grass to grow faster than nature intended. You can accelerate it—fertilize the soil, use the best grass seed, provide enough light and water—but you can't overcome the natural X factor required of all gestation, the time needed to cook till done.

It will take longer than two weeks because you'll probably want to test the crucial elements like your name and DSI tags, even if only for a disaster check. You may need to bring in professional creative talent to boost memorability of the core elements—to help with key visuals, Golden Metaphors, or other points of the star that will require a little extra time to polish.

But most importantly, you'll need to match your new DSI to your specific performance and take stock of what works and what needs to be adjusted, realigned, or invented to produce TCA (Total Consistent Alignment) of your business up, down, and sideways to guarantee DSI-level performance as advertised. Not only will you have to draft your list of elements, you'll have to execute them within the organization. Some may take a week or a month. The master list may take two years, depending on the scope of your makeover. And the ultimate list will never be 100 percent completed, as long as you're in business and your brand is alive and evolving as all great brands must.

Minimum Time to Launch Versus Completing of the DSI Star

The point is, don't fret if parts of the branding process remain open-ended for the time being—for two practical reasons:

1. Remember that you've come 95 percent of the way already. Just by nailing your DSI and your brand story in the past six weeks, you're ahead of most competitors.
2. You don't have to have the whole DSI star finalized to launch your new position into the world, just the minimum parts listed below. A new hotel can get an occupancy permit, even though the landscaping around the pool isn't all done. The hotel doesn't need landscaping to sell rooms, but it does need beds, *capiche*?

Likewise, the minimum to start new messaging is:

Your name

Your specialty statement

Your brand story

Performance capacity that's at least commensurate with your promise—even if you aren't yet capable of exceeding your promises.

You need your new name for obvious reasons. You have no brand without one. You need your specialty statement and your brand story to focus and align your new messaging with your DSI.

You need to be set to perform because nothing will kill you faster than a new, powerful DSI proposition that stimulates trial, then makes the customer feel like a fool and makes you look like a liar. Who hasn't seen that potentially wonderful new restaurant with the great name that opens three weeks too soon, before the staff is trained, coordinated, and ready. In those first three weeks, the whole community shows up excited to try the place. The atmosphere's exciting, the menu looks great. Then it takes an hour to get the first course, the soup's cold, two people at your table get their entrées but the other two never get theirs . . .

The multiplier effect of those lost first impressions, bad references, and general disappointment is brand suicide. The restaurant never recovers.

If you're a software company, wait the extra month to release your new product—until the main bugs are fixed. If you're a new airport in Denver touting world-class convenience and amenities, don't open (or at least don't advertise) until your baggage system is actually working. If you're a mail order catalog claiming superior customer care, make sure that your call center is ready to answer the phone in three rings, not thirteen minutes.

So, assuming you've got your specialty statement and brand story in place, how much more time will you need—minimum—before you can kick your new DSI out of the nest, even if every point of the DSI star isn't totally completed?

The answer—based on twenty-five years of experience, believe it or not, if everything goes right is:

about two more weeks.

(Hey, that's the end of week 8!) Indeed, we have seen a number of companies do it that quickly, but only if and only when:

1. They've got their new name or don't need a name change.
2. They've got their proposed DSI nailed and tested.
3. They've got their minimum requisite DSI-level performance ready—or don't need to change prior performance.
4. They've conducted basic, reasonable tests of the new elements for unintended effects, reactions, surprises and legal availability (trademark or patent infringement)—i.e., they know their new name doesn't mean *moose poop* in Swedish if they have big plans to launch in the Scandinavian market.

So it can be done and it has been done fast—even in multibillion-dollar companies. But don't push it before its time because you'll short circuit yourself. And the bigger and more complex you are as a business, the louder the warning.

To-do List and Tips for the Last Two Weeks
Star Point 1: Naming

Remember how important your name can be to the success of your Dominant Selling Idea. If you're switching specialties, if your present name is losing relevance or has no particular equity (or even negative equity), if you're easily confused with a competitor, if you have a "reason why" process or a unique capability that could be described but currently isn't, or if you've been presented with a resonating humdinger that just popped out during your interview process that's so memorable and appropriate, you can't resist, then *name*.

This goes for products, services, or your company name itself, depending on your brand's focal point. The decision is a no-brainer for new products, of course, and gets more difficult when you're renaming a product or a company that may even offer multiple product lines. And, don't forget that the value of renaming has to exceed the cost of new signage, graphics, materials, and communications, which can be quite considerable the more established you are.

The rule of thumb on timing if you're starting from scratch is this: compiling your initial names list, conducting one or two additional rounds based on feedback, narrowing candidates, getting internal consensus, and simple testing and legal vetting of a new name should take you three to six weeks.

Last-Minute Naming Advice

Our biggest advice is a reminder—be as descriptive, specific, and colorful as you possibly can. We call it the "Invisible Fence" school of naming. The opposite of this and your last, worst resort is the "Meaningless Coined Word or Initials" school of naming: i.e., Attribula, Dipulent, and any set of initials at all.

Sometimes you have no choice but to coin a word—with pharmaceuticals, for instance. But coined words can be excellent and creative when they obviously point to a real descriptor word or combination. *Compaq* computers was great because it was descriptive of compact portability, Compaq's DSI at the time, with a high tech twist.

We've also said we like the name *Viagra*, for example.

Again, a great name will be:

1. A direct statement of, or highly supportive of, your DSI
2. Descriptive, evocative, or colorful in some way
3. Ownable by you
4. Easy or pleasing to say

Finally, here's a simple, commonsense creative technique that's used by everyone from professional namers to Hollywood comedy writers when writing topical jokes:

First, take a blank page. Down the left margin, list every quality, attribute, aspiration, idea, person, place, or thing that comes to mind when you think of the product or company. Be freewheeling and write everything down.

Then circle any that are particularly unique to your product—but don't count out the general words either because sometimes a combination of those best describes something unique.

Next, with the list in the left margin for guidance and inspiration, start creating, combining, and describing in the blank space on the right side of the page. You'll fill the space quicker than you think, so pull out another page and keep going. The difference between finding a great name and a mediocre one is often a matter of not quitting too soon because this is a game of persistence. Just when you think you've burned out every creative spark, the winner will hit you out of nowhere. When you think you've got something, quit for the day and pick your list up in the morning. The ones that hold up overnight have the potential. And don't forget the creative power of the shower.

Star Point 2: Naming Your Specialty

Consider specialty names like: *Mini-Skirt, Mini-Bar, Toilette Water, Sports Car, Wonder Bra, Day Spa, Pope Mobile, Stainless Steel, Air Mattress, Porn Actress, Lip Gloss, Mint Floss, Jumbo Jet, Jumbo-Tron, Litter Box, Fashion Socks, Hot Tub, Toasted Sub, Wine Spritzer, Elliot Spitzer* and recall that our specialty name is different from the descriptive sentences we've already created for our specialty statement. The specialty statement is designed to be accurate and specific first, colorful second—almost like legal language in describing exactly what we're #1 in and why. It's for internal guidance first and foremost, even though it must be clear enough to communicate, if indeed it's seen externally.

Our specialty name, on the other hand, is made with the outside world in mind, and it becomes a point on the DSI star. That's because the more memorable and important a specialty is in its own right, the more valuable our ownership of the #1 spot becomes. And because we know that a customer's mental route to our brand always goes through our specialty first, giving the market a succinct and memorable "handle" improves the odds that customers will direct themselves to our specialty ahead of all the others. We want specialty names to be quick, catchy, descriptive, and appealing—just as we want our product and brand names to be.

Of course, if you're staying in a specialty that already has a suitable specialty name, you don't need to create one. You'll just tack on extenders to separate yourself.

But for those times when you've just designed the perfect car for suburban housewives to drive their commuter husbands to Pleasantville Station, then spend the rest of the day ferrying around kids and sundries, don't call it a Square-backed Suburban Housewife Mobile, call it a Station Wagon. And when Station Wagons become a tired old specialty with dozens of competitors and you've fundamentally reengineered and revitalized the vehicle, enabling a "2 Mints-in-1" DSI template that fuses car and van, call it a Mini-Van. If you've invented a lawn mower–like power appliance that eliminates snow shoveling, call it a Sno-Blower. And if you configure a chain of hotels with extended-stay amenities like kitchens and sitting areas to make business travelers feel more at home than ever, call it a Residence Hotel.

As your specialty gets famous through word of mouth, industry scuttlebutt, and your own messaging, people will seek

Station Wagons, Mini-Vans, and Sno-Blowers as much by your specialty name as your brand name. And that's A-OK when you own the specialty. They'll find you. And the more you satisfy them, the more fame shall befall your brand name.

Star Point 3: DSI Tag Line

We just went back to Chapter 10 on tag lines to remind ourselves of what we've already covered, before continuing here. You know what? You ought to go right back and refresh yourself on Chapter 10, too, because it's all there. Do the practicing, subject your DSI candidates to the tests. Follow the helpful hints, be dogged and persistent, and don't give up until you've expressed a set of words that would make it difficult if not impossible for another competitor to substitute his name for your name and be able to say the same thing.

With a unique and definitive specialty statement that scores a solid three of the five selling ingredients—Superlative, Important, and Believable—you've got all the ingredients to cook a great tag line omelet.

Check your interview notes for lucky pearls of language and phrasing that may already be in your lap.

Express it in the least possible amount of syllables. Sayability is important here, so be conscious that phrasing has different rhythms, some much smoother and more sonorous than others. That's one reason why rhyming is so good, because the meter and the rhythm are built in.

Test your finalists when you're done. If you hire professionals to write your tag, demand that they adhere to the DSI found in the brand story and specialty statement as a key deliverable.

Plan for two to three weeks for first submissions, additional rounds, and basic testing.

Star Point 4: Key Visual

Last-minute words from the coach at game time:

Remember, a key visual is not a graphic identity system like logos and color palettes (which will come later), even though there's no reason why a logo can't utilize your key visual as an element like Merrill Lynch does with its bull and Allstate does with its "good hands." But what we're talking about here is that veritable "picture worth a thousand words" that shows, tells, and proves your DSI in an indelible visual split second. A picture of your selling idea, one of the most powerful selling points of the DSI star:

A lock not failing when shot through by a high-powered rifle,

The magic blurry vapors of Vapor Action going up an actor's nose,

A Bounty paper towel sucking up the whole big spill,

The baby playing in the Michelin tire,

The leathery face of the Marlboro cowboy,

The football bouncing off the Colgate toothpaste "invisible shield,"

The flowers in the meadow for Irish Spring,

The Ginsu knife slicing through a tin can like a pat of butter,

The Nestea plunge,

The Dentyne smile,

. . . and so on.

Some DSIs are inherently more telegenic than others. "Intangible" benefits like the clean, fresh feeling one gets from your brand of soap, or the expertise ones gets from your stock brokers are harder than tangibles like the gunshot wound one *doesn't* get when wearing your brand of bullet-proof vest.

But the Irish Spring meadow and the Merrill Lynch bull show that key visuals can be conceived for less tangible brands, so don't be defeatist.

There's no formula for creating key visuals other than this:

1. Focus on your DSI core.
2. Make all the logical and not-so-logical connections you can.
3. Don't be afraid to be zany, dramatic, and fun.

You, your colleagues, and your in-laws are guaranteed to think of demos, torture tests, and apt metaphors if you keep at it. Follow your thinking all the way through and imagine yourself taking snapshots of the results, looking for the one defining shot that captures the moment of truth—your picture worth a thousand words. Don't hesitate to get professional creative help if visual conceptualizing isn't your forte, as it's not for most of us.

One last thing—of all the points of the DSI star, the time it takes to find your key visual is most difficult to predict. You might get a super idea for a torture test in the first week of your R&D interviews. Or, it may come downstream when a clever art director at your ad agency dreams up a Golden Metaphor for an ad campaign that turns into your iconic image. Marlboro cigarettes were advertised as a woman's cigarette for decades with tag lines like: "Mild as May." The brand virtually died during World War II and was resurrected in the early 1950s. The cowboy wasn't invented until the '60s by the ad agency as just one execution in a general ad campaign that by then featured rugged men in different walks of life, all called "The Marlboro Man." Tests showed the cowboy was so popular, he become the sole visual image for the brand, credited with making Marlboro America's #1-selling cigarette and one of the world's most recognized brands to this day.

All of which is to say, you may or may not come up with your ultimate key visual in the next three or four weeks. If you do find one, it will be enticing icing on your cake. If you don't, you can definitely go to market with your new DSI in the meantime.

But you can definitely *not* go to market without the fifth and final point of the star that follows: DSI-level performance.

Star Point 5: DSI-Level Performance

We'll spare you the speech. This is *the walk*. And by now we all know how important that is. Talk makes you a possibility. Walk makes you a brand.

Creating Total Consistent Alignment (TCA) within your business and your brand, making sure every touch point is enhancing your DSI versus diminishing it, is the most common-sense part of the whole process. It's also the never-ending part. To succeed, you need only follow the Golden Rule: Do unto others as you'd have others do unto you. Step into your customers' shoes and stay there. Ask how exactly would you want to be treated, cared for, talked to, and served to feel that the DSI promise had been delivered to a fair degree? How about to an extraordinary degree? What does TCA look like, sound like, perform like, and behave like when it cascades from top to bottom though the entire organization?

This is not creative brain surgery nor is it beyond anyone's means. The only talent needed is to have been born human and have the willingness to empathize with customers.

What did Richard Branson do to make the experience of Virgin Atlantic Airlines align with the wild, fun, out-of-the-box brand promises of Virgin Enterprises? What did Walt Disney do when he wanted Disneyland to be every bit as pristine, colorful, and magical as the fantasies he'd created in the heads of millions of children for decades? What did Sam Walton do relentlessly, day in and day out, to provide a retail store where "ordinary folk had the chance to buy the same things as rich people"?

Such people never stop thinking about Total Consistent Alignment from the first moment they open their door for business. And they never open the door to begin with until they are sure they can deliver, at the very least, the minimum level of performance commensurate with their DSI.

That last caveat was a prime reason why the dot-comers failed so famously and miserably at the turn of the millennium. Rabid twenty-three–year-olds were permitted to run around screaming for first-to-market share at all costs and spend billions on advertising to capture trial customers—then deliver products that in hundreds of cases were still full of software bugs, lacked minimal customer support, or simply did not work.

So how long will it take for you to line up the requisite DSI-level performance to achieve minimum wattage for the final point of the DSI star?

Plan on three to four weeks from today to have your first punch list of products and services already in place, adjustments that need to be made, and new initiatives that need to be started.

Then only your common sense and good judgment will determine where the minimum hurdle level is to perform as promised, and what resources to allocate in what order of priority. You can be ready to go in three weeks, three months, or more, depending on what needs to be approved, built, and internalized. It will always be a continuous, dynamic process because, after all, DSI-level performance is what your business does.

So don't jump the starting gun. Don't go to market until your DSI is tangible with the minimum requirements for TCA in place.

By the Close of Week 8 . . .

You'll have perspective. You'll have uncovered your Dominant Selling Idea. You'll have inventoried the components of the DSI star already in your possession and assessed the remaining parts to be built before opening your doors to the market.

You'll be able to estimate a realistic time to launch, based on the pace of your creative team's effort, the scope of work, and your initiatives toward minimal, requisite TCA. You'll be on the home stretch and you'll see the finish line, a completed DSI star—the beating heart of a real, idea-centered brand. You'll be on your way to #1 in the minds of your customers.

The End of the Beginning

"Gotta go, gotta go, gotta go right now—Gotta go, gotta go, gotta go . . . !"

Guru Mahatma Mahareshi "Mahesh" Goldberg

Deeply sentimental, as he always is when we arrive at commencement (he calls all of you his "little llamas"), the Guru had to toss a coin between the poignant sign-off above and the timeless opening stanza of "My Way" sung by Elvis. After all, you're about to bid farewell to DSI University and enter the world with a degree that sets you apart from many Madison Avenue executives making two-comma incomes, we must say.

Discovering the DSI mind-set, not to mention your own DSI over the past several weeks, is a big, big milestone for anyone in business. The main battle is truly won or lost at this stage. But it is still just the beginning. You can't rest on your laurels any more than the team that's ahead at the half in the Super Bowl. You've got to finish the game, and the game will test your persistence, courage, ability to withstand being knocked on your butt, tactical skills, and adherence to your central vision before you're done.

In short, you'll be moving from brand origination into brand management—the long-term care, feeding, and watering of an enduring, successful brand.

You'll have a new list of eternal questions to answer, like:

How do I create internal buy-in and maintain commitment and enthusiasm from the inside out?

How do I allocate precious resources?

How do I deal with all the new kinds of media I keep hearing about—like "stealth media" and "viral media" and "grass-roots media"—and how does that affect my messaging?

What's the role of vision and mission statements?

When do I line extend my master brand into subbrands, and how far from my master brand can I credibly go?

How long do I stay with my advertising campaigns or my positioning—my #1 specialty itself—and when should I change?

How do I choose professional help like ad agencies and consultants, and how will I ever know they're giving me my money's worth?

We can't answer these questions for you now because we need enough material for the sequel. And learning to distinguish between idea-centered brands and sponge cake is more than enough for any brand book.

But here are a few parting thoughts to take with you as you go forth to conquer.

When in Doubt, "Arch"

Every sky diver learns this #1 fundamental rule on day one. If you get wobbly in the air, even if you flip upside down by mistake, simply arch your back and you'll immediately right yourself and stabilize. It's the unfailing principle of body flight.

When you're in doubt about your direction, even about downstream strategies like when and how far to credibly line extend, stop and apply your fundamental DSI tests like the five selling ingredients from Chapter 3, the ultimate messaging test from Chapter 5 and the specialty tree from Chapter 6.

Is it Superlative, is it Important, is it Believable (a key when you're line extending), is it Memorable, is it Tangible? Can anyone else substitute their name in place of yours and run the same ad? Are you sharpening your DSI or defusing it?

These tests are your "arch" and they have remarkable focusing power.

DSI First, Vision and Mission Statements After

Beware the Trap

Every business has to start with some kind of "vision." It has to see an opportunity and have an ambition. But the reason you haven't heard us say anything about vision statements and mission statements up to now is that if you try to chisel them in stone before you've positioned yourself with a #1 specialty statement and a DSI, you can put yourself in a major trap.

Vision and mission statements for corporations were made quite popular by consultants over the past few decades, but no one seems to agree on what they are supposed to do or say. We've settled on the notion that your "vision" is what you want to become and your "mission" is what you will do and what you'll provide your customers to get yourself there. Most of the statements we see were undoubtedly written by executive committees who, once they finished including everybody's perfect adjective and affirmative thought, ended up with a broad, flawless, all-encompassing laundry list of aspirations that no one could ever disagree with—but no one could cull a DSI specialty and positioning from, either.

The bottom line on vision is this: it doesn't matter what broad vision you think you have or hope to have, you'd better find the specific vision the market *wants* you to have, that you're capable of having, and that no competitor already has.

DSI branding is about reality. The fine-tuned vision that emerges after you run the gauntlet of the past eight weeks will merge into your DSI. That vision is the kind that can drive a business. That's what our process, starting with R&D, was all about.

Companies who procrastinate from the hard choices of the DSI process by first spending weeks dictating a perfect vision statement often get themselves into a bind. They now feel they have to validate the committee's work by molding their positioning to the vision they've just dreamed up, instead of the other way around. You can't get there from here.

Likewise, mission statements are no more than window dressing unless they point you directly to DSI-level performance and TCA. There's not much point in crafting those either until your DSI is absolutely 100 percent straight in your head beforehand.

So don't put the cart before the horse and try to nail vision and mission language before you've nailed the big idea. Otherwise, those things will inhibit you more than inspire you.

Do Everything You Can to Avoid Being "Creative by Committee"

Everyone's heard the supposed maxim that 90 percent of all new product ideas fail. We once asked Stan Mason, one of America's most renowned full-time inventors (everything from squeezable ketchup bottles to disposable diapers) to comment on that ratio. He said flatly: the only reason 90 percent fail is that corporations get committees together who water down the original creator's vision until it becomes lifeless and useless.

Likewise, our broth gets spoiled with too many cooks. Great creative elements have never been improved in the history of branding by the addition of filter after filter or accommodating layer after layer of input. All you get is a big blender. Remember, everyone feels they have to get credit for adding something to be relevant. They fix and fix and futz and futz until the idea is dead under the weight or at the very least on life support.

If you're in a position to influence the process in your company, do everything in your power not to kill it with too much consensus, especially during the creative stages. Keep the idea-originator group small and give them the most votes when it comes to edits and changes. Subject the ideas to the larger group for feedback and constructive comments—but not for change—unless the originators agree that an adjustment will indeed move the ball forward, not set it back.

And if you're still worried that your minions will be critical if you don't permit creative by group consensus, ask yourself, "What would Leonardo Da Vinci do?"

Have Everyone in Marketing Take a Real Sales Training Course

This can mean reading one or two of the great books, listening to a sales training tape, or attending a brief seminar. One of the main reasons Johnny, the talented folks at ad agencies, and even some marketing consultants can't brand is that they've never been taught by anyone what the Brand Titans, who all started in mail order advertising, knew: every single thing the marketer or brander does should serve one master—*selling*. What we do is selling. Not entertaining, not award winning, not publicity, not commotion, but *selling*. In case that's still not clear, the word is SELLING.

The essential structure of selling—what master salespeople do and many marketing people look down on as déclassé—is a refined art and science that has established rules and techniques that every brand person must embrace on some level to create a real selling brand.

Selling is one of the most specialized forms of communication. It's persuasion—that is, communication with the absolute objective of getting someone to take the action you want.

You've probably heard these terms: *probing; qualifying; identifying needs, features and benefits; objection handling; trial closing;* and *closing*.

These are the mandatory stages for any successful sale. They're simple and immutable.

Which is why we never understood this anomaly: The ad agencies we once worked at used to hire scores of talented, creative kids. The kids would be thrown into the pond and told to swim on day 1, given creative directions, and told to produce advertising ideas for clients.

The day they got hired, these kids thought, "Hey, I just got hired by Ted Bates Worldwide. That means, I'm now an advertising professional."

But not one of these kids had ever sold anything to anyone in his life. Try knocking on some busy person's door who already owns three of whatever it is you're selling and stand there with a quacking duck. But why should those kids have known any better?

Even back then, we swore that when we owned an agency or consultancy someday, we'd make every new hire read at least one of the great selling books and one of the Brand Titans' books to cure this problem. And today we do.

You can too. There are tapes, books, and seminars that will teach you and your people the basic laws of salesmanship in a day. You don't need anything but the classics: sales training books by Dale Carnegie, Brian Tracy, and Tom Hopkins plus the Brand Titan books by John Caples first and foremost, then Victor Schwab and Claude Hopkins. Ultimately Rosser Reeves's *Reality in Advertising*, which goes in and out of print. You can find them online.

There are many others, of course, and these books are not boring. They're fascinating to anyone who wants to know the practical anatomy of the craft and succeed at something beyond barking, meowing, and whistling.

Be Realistic About How Agencies Work

We love advertising agencies and advertising people. They are some of the most talented, professional people in the world.

And when you're hiring them, don't be blind to what motivates them by necessity and design. Now that you understand your DSI objectives as well or better than many of them do, you can better direct their power and creativity to your advantage.

Agencies know they are judged by the outside perception of their creativity. In service of this perception, the industry has established an entire awards system to recognize "great advertising"—translation: funny, entertaining, clever, original and eye-catching. Note that sales revenue and market share are for the most part absent from this awards-qualifying list. Agency creative people get promoted and rewarded for doing the former things—not to mention, it's what they love to do to start with.

So there's always a pull from two directions at agencies: their own understandable business drive to use the client's money to produce "award-winning creative" versus their deeper responsibility to use the client's money to drive sales and market share, a pull that's not always without conflict.

As the one paying the bills, and as a graduate of DSI University, you can help keep this in balance. You want the agency people happy and excited about the work they're doing for you—but you want the two pulls to be in full alignment so that creativity serves sales and share via your DSI, before it puts little statues on the shelf in the art director's den—so that your product is always the star. Smart companies get this kind of creative. There's no reason you can't be one of them.

One Little Rule-of-Thumb Case in Point to Look For

You'll find it's almost the rule, not the exception, that writers will submit ads to you that have clever, eye-catching headlines plus an arresting visual. The headline and key visual are still what provides 80 percent of horsepower in any print ad, because few people will take the time to read the body copy of an ad unless they're enticed by those two big elements up front.

The writer and art director are therefore spending 80 percent of their time on the headline and visual, trying their hardest to be clever and original. Then they get to the chore of writing the body copy, knowing that they have to explain what the heck the product's about, not to mention the meaning of the clever headline, or no one will understand what they're supposed to buy.

Now here's what you will very often find:

The best expression of your DSI and the best words to use as your headline will be found in the body copy that the creative people submit to you in the first round. If you see it, point it out and direct them to come back for the second round with headline treatments that reflect those hidden nuggets.

You'll look like a branding sage. You'll get more communications that advance your DSI. And you'll be getting your money's worth.

All That Said—Don't Be a Bad Client

There is such a thing as a bad client—a client who hires excellent professional creative people, then demands so much control, allows so little free rein, and makes so many unnecessary changes that the agency never hits its creative stride. He stifles them until all they do is regurgitate what he wants until they get an approval, rather than adding the true creative spark that they're capable of and he's paying them for.

Be a wise and reasonable client. As long as your eye is on the "big picture," let them generate the pictures.

If you feel you're always having to grab the wheel to keep your bus on the DSI track, it might be time to look for another agency.

New Mediums Will Come and Go, but DSIs Are Forever

Some people are announcing the end of advertising as we know it, which generally means the end of marketing communications focused strictly on the thirty-second TV commercial. There used to be three mediums: broadcast, print, and direct mail. Now there seem to be new ones popping up every day—everything from the Internet to wireless text messages, viral marketing schemes, stealth tactics where paid "civilians" engage strangers with faux word of mouth, and product placements everywhere you look.

Friends, all this means is that a DSI is more crucial than ever to provide a big idea anchor in this sea of chaos. Remember, every example above is a medium, not a message, not a brand. Whether you're paying a couple of ringers to organize basketball games in Central Park and then sit around showing off their hot new basketball shoes, or you're seeding text message chain mail, ultimately someone has to make a decision to trade their dollars for ownership of your product. Then they have to be pleased with it and remember you for next time. That will always happen best when you've got a name attached to a real Dominant Selling Idea.

And Finally . . .

Andy Rooney said this once on *60 Minutes:*

> "What we need today is less marketing
> and more quality."

We loved hearing him say that. As professional marketers, we must all heed the pithy wisdom of those simple words.

Make genuine performance, service, trustworthiness, fair dealings, helpful innovation, and improving the life of every customer the soul of your brand. Make your vision nothing more than to be the very best you can be at what you'll do. Make your mission to do it the right way always. Then light up the night with your Dominant Selling Idea and the world will beat a path to your door.

INDEX

658.827
Schley   Schley, Bill

        Why Johnny can't
        brand

DUE DATE

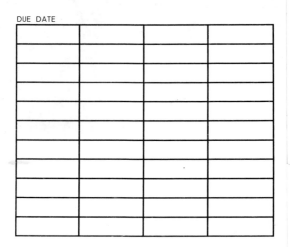